THREE RUSSIAN PROPHETS

BY THE SAME AUTHOR

Moscow, the Third Rome
St. Sergius: Builder of Russia
The Church of the Eastern Christians

DOSTOEVSKY

THREE
RUSSIAN
PROPHETS

KHOMIAKOV

DOSTOEVSKY

SOLOVIEV 1973.

NICOLAS ZERNOV

Third Edition

with a

PREFACE

by the author

ACADEMIC INTERNATIONAL PRESS

1973

The substance of these chapters formed the basis of a course of lectures which was delivered at the School of Slavonic Studies in Oxford and London in 1942. In recasting this material for publication, I have received from the Rev. Patrick Thompson invaluable help, which I am glad to acknowledge here. I am also most grateful to Miss Grace Keeble and Miss Florence Steinberg for their assistance in typing and correcting the manuscript.

N. Z.

Northwood

23·6·43

THE RUSSIAN SERIES/ Volume 23

Nicolas Zernov THREE RUSSIAN PROPHETS
KHOMIAKOV, DOSTOEVSKY, SOLOVIEV

Third Edition. Reimpression of the London edition
of 1944 with a Preface by Nicolas Zernov added

Library of Congress Catalog Card Number: 72-97040
ISBN 0-87569-050-5
A Catalog Card follows the Table of Contents

Copyright©1973 by Academic International Press

Printed in the United States of America

ACADEMIC INTERNATIONAL PRESS
Box 555 Gulf Breeze, Florida 32561

CONTENTS

Zernov, Nicolas, 1898—

    Three Russian prophets: Khomiakov, Dostoevsky, Soloviev. 3rd ed. with a preface by the author. Gulf Breeze, Florida; Academic International Press, 1973.

    xiv, 171 p. ports. 22 cm. (The Russian Series, vol. 23)
    "The basis of a course of lectures. . . delivered at the School of Slavonic Studies in Oxford and London in 1942."

    Reprint of the 1944 ed.
    Bibliography: p. [169]-171.

    1. Khomiakov, Aleksei Stepanovich, 1804-1860. 2. Dostoevskii, Fedor Mikhailovich, 1821-1881. 3. Solovev, Vladimir Sergeevich, 1853-1900. 4. Religious thought—Russia.
I. Title

BX595.Z4 1973   281.947   72-97040

ISBN: 0-87569-050-5

PREFACE

Three Russian Prophets was written in 1942, when the outcome of the Second World War was far from being decided. On some important points the underlying convictions of the book clashed sharply with the mood prevalent in England at that time. Hitler and Nazism were then regarded by the majority as the archenemies of the free world and it was widely believed that their downfall would bring the era of Totalitarianism to an end.

The outlook expressed in the book was much less optimistic. It was based on the conviction that the Christian West was passing through a deep spiritual crisis and that Totalitarianism was only one of its most sinister symptoms. This disease was related to the loss of communion with the living God by so many formal Christians. Atheists, blind to the reality of God, were victims of dreams and illusions and were therefore favourable ground for the false teachers promising them earthly paradise. Western man, who so optimistically started on the triumphant road towards technological progress and material prosperity and who imposed his civilization upon the rest of mankind, was originally inspired by the vision of himself as a redeemed sinner who was called by his Creator to Sonship and collaboration. Human pride, however, alienated men from God. The dark forces of greed and aggression poisoned their minds. The man of the West lost his self-confidence. The attraction to Totalitarianism was not a passing aberration, but a persistent temptation of an emancipated people. They felt lost in the vast impersonal universe which had, according to them, no creator and no purpose. They were prepared therefore, to surrender their freedom to an "infallible" leader in return for promised security and comfort.

This was the main thesis of the book, the purpose of which was to analyse the causes of Christian decline and to suggest the ways of renewal.

Christian disunity, breeding prejudices, suspicions and
sectarianism, was one of the major factors in the decrease of
religious vitality. The impoverishment of spiritual life had many
social and political repercussions. Men have always been potential
rebels against their Creator; the success of technological civilization provided them with new weapons; Communism became the
most powerful expression of men's determination to proclaim
themselves the masters of their own destiny. Ulianov-Lenin captured the imagination of many millions of his followers by the
intensity of his hatred of God and by his determination to liquidate
those who dared to challenge his authority. He became the great
founder of Totalitarianism. His aim was to obliterate all traces of
Christianity, which he considered, rightly, incompatible with
the tenets of his new religion of divinised collectivity.

Russia therefore, not Germany, Leninism, not Nazism, stood
in the centre of confrontation between the Christian and Totalitarian outlooks. The Russian people were such a vital factor in
this spiritual combat because, besides the Communists, they had
also a vigorous Christian community, which remained undestroyed
in spite of the most cruel and persistent persecution ever known
to mankind. The Russian Orthodox Church is in many respects
different from Western confessions. Yet its interpretation of
Christianity is complementary both to Rome and Protestantism.
The restoration of communion between the East and the West
is an indispensable condition for the invigoration of the Church
and for the expansion of Christian culture.

The Russian Orthodox occupy the same key position in the
Ecumenical movement which the Russian Leninists hold in international Communism.

The vital role of Russia in the present critical state of mankind
was foreseen by the great Russian religious thinkers of the XIX
century. These men had a prophetic insight into the future. The
study of their works helps to understand the roots of Totalitarianism and the ways of overcoming this distortion of the secular man.

Such were some of the suggestions around which the book
was written thirty years ago. It is appropriate to re-examine them
in the light of the events which have taken place since its first
publication.

It appears that some of the ideas expressed in the book have
been confirmed; others are still open to debate. So, for instance,
it is obvious now that the victory over Nazism did not eliminate
the danger of Totalitarianism. On the contrary, it brought about

its expansion over the major parts of Europe and Asia. Paradoxically the Western allies who started the war in order to defend the independence of Poland and Czechoslovakia, delivered these countries into the custody of the archdespot, Stalin.

The end of Western domination over Asia and Africa, foreseen in the book, was equally achieved, and even quicker and more radically than could have been anticipated.

The book's insistence that the present malaise of Western society with its fixation on sex, drug addiction and blind violence and destruction, has its roots in religion, has also been affirmed, for it is provoked not by poverty but by material prosperity.

The post war history of Christianity presents a more baffling and complex picture. Neither revival nor decline has taken place. The most dramatic and the least expected change has occurred in the Roman Church. After centuries of immobility and unflexing conservatism, its adherents embarked on a daring road of renovation and revision. Much confusion followed; many clergy and members of religious Orders deserted their ranks. At the same time a new creative Spirit animates the community. The Roman Catholics and other Christians have improved their relations and strengthened the sense of their unity.

The destiny of the Russian Church presents also a puzzling and contradictory picture. On the eve of Germany's attack on Poland, Stalin claimed complete victory over the Christians. Only some few hundreds of churches were still opened in his vast domains and even these were on the point of being closed down. Yet the same Stalin made a spectacular retreat on the religious front, where he was particularly sure of triumph. On the 4th of September, 1943, he concluded a concordat with three bishops who managed to survive outside the concentration camps and walls of prison. As a result of this, ten years later the Russian Church presided over by the Patriarch Alexis (1944-70) had some seventy bishops, thirty thousand priests, twenty-two thousand parishes, eight theological schools and several monasteries and convents.

The Church rose from its death bed. Though strictly controlled by the party officials it was no longer molested. Stalin, who always betrayed others, this time, to the great surprise of everybody, kept faithfully until his death the concordat with Church leaders.

The period of expansion was, however, drastically interrupted by Krushchev. As soon as he consolidated his power, he released a new wave of persecution. By 1962 the number of parishes was

halved to eleven thousand, only fourteen thousand priests were
allowed to exercise their ministry and only three theological
schools remained open. But the last persecution differed from the
earlier ones organised by Lenin and Stalin. It was almost blood-
less. The Christians were harassed, oppressed, expelled, but only
a few of them were murdered.

As a résult of this new trial the Russian Church presents an
ambiguous picture. Inside the country it functions on a
diminishing scale. In contrast, outside Russia it takes an increasingly active part in international conferences and discussions.
Its official representatives declare their complete satisfaction with
the conditions imposed upon them by the atheist government and
even express their gratitude for its help and protection.

These declarations are, nonetheless, contradicted by other
voices heard from time to time from Russia. These describe the
sufferings and dangers to which the faithful believers are exposed.
One fact remains well established. The Church has stood firm once
more under the devastating outburst of the rage of Communists.
Under these adverse conditions all the negotiations with the West
must remain suspended. Only when the Church is free from secular
control can reconciliation be achieved.

The official voice of the Russian Church is unable to express
the true mind of the Russian congregation at present. In the nineteenth century for other reasons the prophets of the Russian
Church were also lay members and were not the authorised
spokesmen of the Church. They were misunderstood and ignored
by their contemporaries, but they found gifted disciples on the eve
of the collapse of the Russian Empire when a group of outstanding
Russian intellectuals exchanged their Marxism for Christianity
and joined the Orthodox Church.* Some of these converts took
refuge in the free world and the writings of men like Berdyaev,
Bulgakov, Frank and others contributed greatly to the deeper
understanding of the Christian faith. Their works are strictly forbidden in Russia, but the intellectual elite of the country, with
increasing attention, studies them and learns from them.

Russia remains the testing ground for the opposing forces
of Christianity and atheistic Totalitarianism and this is even
more so today than it was thirty years ago. Much of this struggle

---

* The story of their conversion is told in my book *The Russian Religious
Renaissance of the XX Centruy* (London: Darton, Longman & Todd, 1963).

is still concealed from the sight of the Christian West, the destiny of which nevertheless is bound to the fate of the Christian community in Russia. This is the main message of this book and the post-war years have confirmed this underlying conviction more explicitly than could have been expected.

N. Zernov

January 1973
Oxford

Introduction

RUSSIA AND THE CHANGING WEST

RUSSIA to-day attracts the attention of the whole world. Admired or feared, she cannot be ignored. Changes that for other nations are still no more than tendency or experiment, in Russia appear as commitments recklessly accepted, achievements ruthlessly pushed through.

After centuries of isolation, Russia stands at the centre of the clash of arms and of ideas. The trials her people have gone through during their long withdrawal have prepared them to take the lead in that search for a new order which alone unites a warring world. For the wars and revolutions of the twentieth century mark the end of the domination of that liberal humanistic culture which Western Europe and its offshoot in North America have imposed upon contemporary mankind.

For the last four hundred years Europe, economically and spiritually, has ruled the globe. No challenge has been offered to Western man's conviction of the superiority of his own beliefs and institutions. The "white man's burden" was his own measure of the white man's stature. By the end of the nineteenth century European ascendancy was so complete that the future of mankind was viewed on the assumption that all nations would gladly adopt Western civilisation in general, and parliamentary government in particular. Ancient cultures, long distinct and independent, had everywhere been economically constrained to come to terms with the self-confident and enterprising spirit of the West.

But the wider Western domination spread, the more clearly

did the defects of this spirit show. The twentieth century has seen a sudden flagging of its energy and faltering of its self-confidence. The self-appointed leaders of mankind stand at a loss. The Western nations are jealous of each other, and the rest of the world is jealous of their common pretensions. But war and unrest have been no more than symptoms of a deeper breaking-up. The root of the trouble lies in the faulty notion of man held in the West, and spread with its arms and wares.

European culture has been shaped by the belief that man is a rational and free being, whose needs and wishes can and should mould the world.

The origin of this conviction lies deep in Christian faith. Man, though a fallen sinner, is yet a child of God, and may become the friend and fellow worker of the Maker of all things. This belief, which set Christians free from the paralysing fascination of Fate and Chance, lent them new energy and courage. But the elements from which it was woven have been torn apart and used to destroy one another. Now, original sin, which makes man's achievements provisional and precarious, is forgotten. God, once man's goal and guide, ground of his being and source of his power, has shrunk to "the Spirit of Man"—his better self. Man finds himself alone, persuaded now that his own abilities are all the grace, his own devices all the bliss, that he can hope for or requires.

Thus in Europe was born the new, emancipated man, master of his own destiny. At the Renaissance it was the freedom of man which was stressed. God still seemed close, and friendly, only somewhat less exacting than had been supposed. By the eighteenth century the rationality of man bulked larger. God was by then so far away that it had become possible to patronise Him. He could still be useful, and might be respected, if He would learn to keep His place. God stoked the fires, but man was at the wheel. With the nineteenth century the development of the natural sciences finally made God superfluous, and seemed to promise man the succession to the office of Providence, if not to that of Creator. But the very discoveries that banished God at the same time sapped man's belief in his own rationality and freedom. Western man saw himself as an animal, distinguished only by the ingenuity with which he resisted the blind hostility of Nature, and by the sensitivity which made his recognition of the ultimate futility of his efforts a torture to him. Physics and chemistry, history and biology, each in turn proved chapters, not of a new Genesis or even a new Job, but of a new Ecclesiastes.

Economics and psychology completed the process of disenchantment. Karl Marx and Sigmund Freud between them, through their popularisers, have coloured the imagination of twentieth-century Europe, and left a picture of man from which the last traces of the image of God in human freedom and rationality have disappeared. Fate and Chance rise again in the shape of economic materialism and psychological determinism. The rational forms of public and private life, politics, philosophy, art, love, virtue and religion seem only illusive shadows cast by the blind movements of dark, subhuman forces.

No wonder Western man shows a loss of nerve, and looks incapable of holding the conquests he had won in the strength of his former belief in himself and his own powers. Talk of a civilising mission rings hollow in his ears, and nation after nation has despaired of ordering its own life by rational debate, and resigned itself to the despotism of a dictatorship which promised at least to hold the herd together in the struggle for pasture grounds. Because the herds of Asia are larger and as yet less sicklied o'er with the pale cast of thought, there were even found thinkers to preach resignation to their inevitable succession to the dominance of the West.

But the whole of the West is still far from accepting the message of these prophets of pessimism, and energetic voices have been raised to contradict it. Western man is impotent, it is claimed, merely because he has bemused himself with errors, not because his stock is dying, and his original faith proved false.

Events have demonstrated beyond denial the dependence of action on belief—not the belief subscribed to in creeds and covenants and constitutions, but that held in men's hearts and revealed by their behaviour. In order to go forward in action it is now necessary to go back to the belief which once made and could again make action vigorous and fruitful.

For good or ill, the tutelage of the rest of the world to Western Europe is ended. The other races and cultures have been brought to self-awareness and maturity in a hard school, and it is only in free collaboration with them that now the West can hope effectively to relearn the purpose of man in the world, and of men in community. The economic interdependence which the West has imposed upon mankind demands a political unification to correspond with it; and that in its turn can only be a worldwide tyranny if it is not the natural expression of a spiritual and cultural unity. We have chosen to build the roof of the house first, and we cannot complain if it is draughty till the walls and the floor are supplied.

The Western nations are no longer specifically Christian. The other nations are not Christian yet. There remains, under the uniform veneer of Westernised civilisation, a great diversity of cultures, governed by the various religious backgrounds of Latin, Orthodox, and Protestant Christianity, of Judaism, Islam and Hinduism. A free association of peoples with such different traditions and such uniform needs demands such mutual trust, forbearance and consideration as only a freely accepted common belief can supply. Where can such a belief be found? It is the great question of our time: and the answer which Russian experience and reflection would suggest to it is worthy of attention.

For Russia is not, like Germany, France or Italy, a national state. It is a cultural unity embracing a number of different races and nations. Yet its cohesion has always depended on the common outlook upon life of the dominant majority, the Russians proper; and that in its turn has been shaped by one factor above all, Orthodox Christianity. This was the form of the old Russia: and the old Russia is the foundation of the new. Russia is a unity much more akin to India, China or Islam than to a modern European national state. Like India and China, it is a culture of peasant communities. Like Islam, it does not recognise state barriers and asserts the brotherhood and equality of all the faithful.

In Europe, geography dictated the boundaries of the cultural units, and provided for a diversity within it. The Græco-Roman sources of European religion and polity ensured that this original diversity would be preserved and accentuated. Europe has remained a Balance of Powers, and the typical European polity is a balance of interests like that network of city-states and colonies which constituted the Roman Empire. Russia, lacking internal frontiers, and ignoring the analytic and particularising tendencies of Græco-Roman thought and jurisprudence, has remained a much more fluid entity. The Western mind has been pre-occupied with drawing boundaries, the Russian mind with looking for the core of things.

The field, and the instruments, of investigation have been different too. The field of investigation which the Russians have made their own has been that of the twin problems of personal integrity and of the relation between the individual and community. The instruments which by preference they have employed have been the plastic arts, fiction, and the ritual of common daily life, all notably more intuitive than intellectual, more communal than individual. The Russians have sought truth and righteousness rather in "living life" than in codes or concepts.

The importance of these distinctions is that Russian culture, Christian but not European, 'is the providential mediator and interpreter between the two worlds of Europe and Asia on whose mutual understanding, sympathy and collaboration the peaceful future of the globe depends. Is it too much to hope that both Europe and Russia, after their experiences of the last twenty-five years, are in sufficiently chastened mood to listen to, and learn from, one another? The shocks, sufferings and disappointments of the present time suggest the possibility of their co-operation, but it is necessary to recognise that the obstacles are still great.

There remains from the isolation and the betrayals of the past some actual hostility, much vague suspicion, and an enormous amount of sheer bewilderment. The conduct and character of the Russians often seems to present to a Western mind a bundle of contradictions. They are devout to the edge of superstition, and godless to the point of persecution; introspective and visionary, hard-headed and capable; anarchical and servile; much-enduring and violent.

The clue to these puzzles is Russian history; and Russian history will be misunderstood so long as Russian Christianity is ignored. Western Europeans have long remained culpably ignorant of Russian background, whilst Westernised Russians despised and misinterpreted their own Orthodox Church. There is no excuse for either class to-day.

Within the last hundred years several Russian Christian writers have been at work trying to specify the culture and the mission of Russia by the easiest and most obvious method, that of comparison and contrast with the culture and destiny of Western Christendom. It is the purpose of this book to introduce Western readers to the thought on this theme of three of the greatest of such writers, Khomiakov, who died in 1860, Dostoevsky, who died in 1881, and Soloviev, who died in 1900. Their upbringing, circumstances and temperament were strikingly different. The first was an amateur publicist, the second a professional novelist and journalist, the third an academic philosopher. Yet their thought shows an impressive convergence and development. Khomiakov was the first to disclose the individuality and greatness of Russian Christianity to the mind of educated Western man, and he did so almost solely by way of contrast and contradictions

Dostoevsky felt and conveyed with almost equal force the attraction and repulsion of godless Europe for believing Russia. Soloviev pointed the way to the reconciliation of Eastern and Western Christendom, of science and revelation.

All three saw so deeply into the realities of their own day and of the past that much of what they had to say has been verified only in our own time; it was in form an interpretation of Russia, it is in substance an interpretation of man: and it is a deeper understanding of the nature and destiny of man that is the most valuable lesson Europe has to learn from the Russian Christian tradition.

Chapter One

THE RUSSIAN BACKGROUND

THE birth of Russian culture dates from 988, the year when missionaries from Constantinople brought the message of the Eastern Orthodox Church to the people of Kiev and Novgorod. The Orthodox Church became the centre round which the various tribes and races inhabiting the Russian plain were to find their spiritual unity and that distinctive outlook which is what we really mean when we speak of "Russia." Many factors contributed towards the originality of Russian culture; the climate and geography of the Russo-Siberian plain, the mixture of Slavonic, Finnish and Mongolian blood among its inhabitants, the special circumstances under which the Christian religion was brought to its people, and, finally, their history, which cut them off for several centuries from the rest of Christendom.

The Russo-Siberian plain is the largest in the world, covering one-sixth of the land's surface. Conventionally this plain is divided by the Ural Mountains into European Russia and Asiatic Siberia, but in reality it forms geographically and climatically one unit. Some modern Russian historians even call the country "Eurasia," for Russia is distinct both from Europe and Asia, and is a continent by itself. The most important characteristic of these huge open spaces is their isolation from the rest of the world. Russia is more cut off from her neighbours than any country with the exception of Tibet. This may seem strange at first sight, for Russia has one of the longest coastlines, and her land boundaries extend from China to Norway. Yet this enormous frontier is more like a prison wall than a gateway. Russia's northern frontier is ice-bound even in summer, and only in the last few years has navigation become possible there. Her southern frontier is formed by some of the highest and wildest mountains, beyond which lie the deserts of Mongolia and Tibet. Equally inhospitable and inaccessible is the eastern boundary of the plain, consisting of the little explored mountains of the Stonovoi range and the Sea of

B

Okhotsk. The only two accessible sea outlets into the wider world are found in the west, and these are the Black and Baltic Seas. Unfortunately, however, they both end in narrows which have always been in the hands of Russia's enemies, and even the control of the Russian shores of these seas was for many centuries denied to the Russian people.

The rest of the western frontier is marshy or mountainous, and the few suitable passages between Russia and Europe have always been firmly held by unfriendly and suspicious neighbours.

Thus Russia, in spite of its extended sea and land frontiers, has no easy line of communication with other countries, and its isolation is still as real in the twentieth century as it has been in the past.

It is necessary to spend some time on that plain to realise how completely its inhabitants are cut off from the rest of the world. The vast majority of them never reach the limits of their land, and have no knowledge of the countries which lie beyond its inaccessible borders.

There is, however, a strange paradox about this Russian isolation, for it offers no protection from attack. It is singularly difficult to get out of Eurasia, but it is equally easy to invade it. Those who could seize the control of the ways leading into it could penetrate without hindrance into its open, exposed spaces. The scattered population, without any natural line of self-defence, presents an easy prey to a determined invader, who can strike at the time and place he chooses. Situated between the warlike nomads of the high plateaux of Asia and aggressive western neighbours, the Russians have suffered from constant incursions of hostile armies; and whilst they could seldom hit back at their enemies, their own country has been regularly laid waste by the intruders.

So it can be said that the whole history of Russia is dominated by two outstanding factors: the scarcity of friendly contacts with the outside world, and the constant threat of sudden invasion by one or other of its neighbours. Thus, from the geographical point of view, Russia can be described as the very opposite of Great Britain—an island whose inhabitants have free access to all parts of the world, whilst they themselves are singularly well protected from the attacks of enemies by a narrow but deep stretch of sea.

The Russian climate is hard and less favourable to the growth of culture than the moderate and more friendly seasons of Western Europe. Its sharp contrasts impose upon its inhabitants a long period of enforced inactivity, followed by outbursts of the most strenuous work. There are some months in the winter when men can do nothing, and there are hours in the summer on which hang the success or failure of the harvest, and this means life or death for those who depend entirely upon it. Its most striking characteristic is the sudden change from the stillness and deadly grip of the winter to the awakening of Nature in the spring. After six months of snow and ice, the Russian plain comes back to life almost overnight. The spring floods rush with noise and clamour, green grass appears everywhere, birds start singing. Nature reveals its hidden power, and it deeply impresses the human soul with its message of resurrection and transfiguration.

If the seasons in Russia are strongly marked, the landscape on the contrary is gentle. There is nothing arresting to the eye about it; Russia is a flat, slightly undulating country, open or wooded, crossed by big, slow-moving rivers. The plain is everywhere the same, and yet never truly monotonous; the same scenery, though repeated over and over again, has a freshness and charm like the ever-moving waves of the ocean. Like the sea, Russia lies open in all directions; it seems to have no end; there is nothing to stop a man from moving further and further afield once he has started on his journey. It invites the adventurous spirit to search the unknown, for profit or for luck. But, like the ocean, it has also its own dangers. It presents an open road to friend and foe alike, and affords no protection to those who are caught unaware in the midst of its sudden storms. Those who live on that plain have acquired characteristics which are not to be found among the inhabitants of better sheltered parts of the world. For generations the people of Russia have been on the move, and this applies not only to the nomads of the south and of the extreme north, but even to the agricultural population of the central regions. Till the end of the eighteenth century, the Russians who lived on the fertile soil of the steppes suffered from the constant danger of hostile incursions. At any moment their homes and fields might be devastated, and a man was never certain whether next year he would toil on the same piece of land or have to escape to another part of the country. Further north, amongst the forests and swamps, the population was more secure, but there the hungry soil would not repay more than a few years' cultivation.

There, every four or five years, a Russian had to move further afield, abandoning his temporary dwelling in search of more promising virgin soil. So the conditions of life on the Russian plain made people sit loosely to their earthly possessions,—its inhabitants were used to hardships, dangers and privations unknown to the people of Western Europe. The Russians are accustomed to the heat of the summer, and the intense cold of the winter; they can display an astonishing degree of energy, enterprise and perseverance, but the periods of intense work are necessarily followed by spells of idleness and inactivity. A Russian must often feel helpless in face of the power of Nature. The winter snow-storms are terrifying, the floods of the spring respect no barriers, the periodic droughts are still beyond human control, and the only attitude which man can take in face of these manifestations of Nature is resignation. But, though Nature in Russia favours man less than in western Europe, it would be quite wrong to represent it as inimical to human beings. On the contrary, the Russian landscape, save in sudden outburst of winter blizzards, is serene and peaceful. Its colours are fresh and harmonious, and its sounds and scents are soft and pleasing. The Russians feel profound and tender attachment to their land; indeed, they speak of the earth itself as "Mother," and Nature in Russia neither crushes man by its majesty and power nor spoils him by the abundance of its gifts; it provides him with sufficient means of existence, if he is willing to work hard and has enough endurance to await the results of his labour in faith. There is something ascetic and supremely simple about the Russian landscape. It neither excites nor enfeebles man, but helps him to understand himself and to find harmony and peace. Like the sea, the Russian plain is dominated by the sky; one can never forget its constant presence there; the sky in Russia seems very close to the earth. The psychology of the Russian people and the character of their culture have been profoundly influenced by the landscape and climate of their plain. Many contradictions in their temperament are to be found in the land they have inhabited from the start of their history. The Russian plain is both severe and gentle; it is hospitable, yet full of concealed dangers; its rivers are friendly and welcoming, but its marshes and forests are threatening and forbidding; it knows how to attach man to the soil, and yet it constantly reminds him of eternity and heaven.

The Russian plain has been inhabited from the dawn of human history. Its pastures presented great attractions to the warlike peoples emerging from the depths of Asia, but none of them managed to establish a permanent home there till it became the abode of the Slavonic nation. Its first appearance in Russia occurred in the second century A.D., but it is only in the fifth century that the Byzantine chronicles describe the south of Russia as wholly inhabited by Slavs. The Greeks represented them as a virile race, divided into numerous, always quarrelling tribes. They greatly surprised the Byzantine historians, for they kept no slaves, and, if they took prisoners, allowed them to settle down among themselves as equals. The information supplied by the Greek writers about the early history of the Slavs is scarce and insufficient for any detailed picture of their life. It seems, however, that the Slavonic tribes were less ferocious than their neighbours, that they had no kings with wide power, but that their clans were ruled on a democratic basis. Men and women enjoyed equality and were entitled to perform religious ceremonies. They lacked temples and an organised priesthood, and worshipped divine power revealing itself through the various manifestations of Nature. The sun, moon, wind, earth, and especially the thunderstorm, were considered by the Slavs to be the vehicles of divinity. They also venerated the spirits of their ancestors, and believed that woods, rivers, lakes and houses were inhabited by benevolent as well as malignant spirits. One of their most important customs was the funeral feast on the tomb of the departed, which perpetuated the fellowship between dead and living and strengthened the family bonds among those who took part in it.

Love of independence and the lack of centralised authority were the causes of their military weakness; though brave and good fighters, they were often subjugated by better disciplined neighbours. Their chief occupation was agriculture, supplemented by hunting and the collection of honey.

From the fifth century the Danubian Basin, a large part of the Balkan peninsula, the north-eastern part of Germany up to the River Elbe, the Carpathian Mountains, and the valley of the Dnieper were the home of Slavonic people. The eastern branch of the Slavs, gradually expanding towards north and north-east, had taken a leading part in the creation of the Russian culture and provided it with its literary language.

While the south of Russia remained the scene of never-ceasing clashes among rival invaders, the thick forests of the north afforded refuge to a number of small tribes, mostly of Finnish origin, which were pushed thither by more warlike and stronger neighbours. Stubbornly clinging to their paganism, living chiefly as hunters, these people formed another racial stratum, which took part, though to a large extent passively, in the shaping of the Russian culture. Various Asiatic nomads, especially the Tartars, were yet another factor contributing to its growth. These diverse nationalities, which originally had nothing in common religiously, linguistically or racially, were moulded into one body, because the Russo-Siberian plain held them in contact with the Slavs, who outnumbered them and were themselves shaped by a single religion. The Russian interpretation of Byzantine Christianity is in that sense the true creative source of Russian culture, which owes to it most of its specific characteristics.

Christianity was brought to the inhabitants of the Russo-Siberian plain at the end of the tenth century. At that time Russia experienced one of her few periods of close co-operation with the wider world, her big rivers, such as the Dnieper and the Volga, were the main commercial routes between Europe and Asia. Kiev and Novgorod, the two chief cities of the country, were important international centres of trade, and these ties brought their enterprising inhabitants in close touch with the main religious traditions of the Mediterranean world,—the Eastern orthodoxy of the Greeks, the Latin Christianity of the Germans and Scandinavians, the Islam of the Arabs and the Judaism professed by the powerful community of the Khazars, whose empire extended over the steppes along the Volga and the Don. According to the story told by the chronicle, Russians accepted Christianity of their own choice. The chronicle relates that Vladimir, Prince of Kiev (d. 1015), after consulting the elders of the land sent out ten wise men to the neighbouring states in order to investigate which was the best religion professed by them. On their return, the delegates unanimously declared that nothing impressed them more than the celebration of the Holy Eucharist at St. Sophia in Constantinople. The beauty and splendour of that worship was so magnificent that the Russian envoys did not know whether they were still on earth or already in heaven. This narrative so moved Prince Vladimir and the members of his Council that they decided to join the Eastern Orthodox Church.

Even if the historical accuracy of the whole episode may legitimately be doubted, it contains a deep symbolic truth. The Russians from the very start of their history have been particularly sensitive to beauty. Worship and its artistic perfection have always been their primary concern. It is therefore not by chance that the national chronicle points to the æsthetic quality of the Byzantine liturgy as the chief reason for Vladimir's preference of Eastern Orthodoxy to all other forms of religion.

The solemn baptism of Prince Vladimir, known as the Bright Sun, and of his family was followed by the conversion of many leading citizens of Kiev and other principal towns. Later on large numbers of the common people were summarily instructed, and baptised in streams and rivers. From the chronicle it appears that the propagation of the new faith aroused but little resentment. The opposition was local and spasmodic: the majority of the Slavs did not find it difficult to embrace Christianity. The Finnish population reacted differently, and their hostility to the Church was stubborn and lasting. Two factors facilitated the acceptance by the Russians of the faith in Jesus Christ. One was their own religious background, which was in many ways congenial to Christianity. The other was the fact that, unlike most European countries, the Russians were offered the liturgy and the Scriptures in the language familiar to them.

The Byzantine Church, when it was called to evangelise the Russian people, was not at the height of its spiritual power. The political decline of the Empire, the increasing hostility between Eastern and Western Christians, the conquest by the Moslems of the centres of ancient civilisation in Syria, Egypt and Palestine— all these factors unfavourably affected the life of the Byzantine Church. Yet, in spite of all, it still presented the most balanced and complete revelation of Christian truth available at the period. Its doctrine was sound. Its understanding of man incorporated in the writings of the great ascetics and Fathers was profound and genuine. Its liturgy contained some of the highest achievements of religious art. Its churches were unsurpassed in beauty and splendour. The Byzantine Church of the tenth century was linked by a direct, uninterrupted line of development to the Church of the Apostles and the great Œcumenical Councils. It possessed an intimate knowledge of the classical civilisation, and it incorporated into its ritual and customs much of the wisdom and experience of the ancient Oriental world. Many of the spiritual treasures created by the Mediterranean peoples from the beginning of their civilisation were carefully preserved in the storehouse of Eastern Christianity, and though they were not always widely used, they were still revered and appreciated by its more enlightened members.

This Church, with all its rich past, was, however, open to new movements, and its adoption of the Slavonic tongue for missionary purposes in the ninth century was a sign of its enterprise and vigour.

Two of its outstanding missionaries, the brothers Cyril (*d.* 869) and Methodius (*d.* 885), are credited with having invented the Slavonic alphabet, and translated into that language some of the most important portions of the Bible and Church service books. Their mission was originally confined to Moravia, but after the brothers' death their disciples, persecuted by the Germans, who strongly objected to the creation of a Slavonic-speaking Church in the centre of Europe, found their way to Bulgaria and continued the work of evangelism there. Thus when Prince Vladimir asked for priests for Russia, the Byzantine Church was able to dispatch men who could preach the word of God, and celebrate the services, in a tongue understood by the Slavs.

Among many causes which have contributed to Russia's isolation and led her to create a culture widely different from that of the rest of Europe, the most important has been the use of the Slavonic tongue in worship and teaching. This cultural separation may be regarded as a blessing or an evil, but the fact remains that Russia, though Christianised, was only loosely connected with her mother Church of Byzantium, and even more drastically cut off from the life and thought of the West. Scholasticism, Renaissance, Reformation and Counter-reformation all lay outside Russia's interests; her neighbours have followed lines of thought which seem at no point to intersect her own. Plato and Aristotle, Virgil and Cicero were the teachers of Byzantine and Latin Christians alike, and their authority not infrequently competed with that of the Doctors and Fathers of the Church, but their influence never reached Russian soil. Russia, although incorporated into the society of Christian nations, has remained a very peculiar member of it. Till Peter the Great's reforms at the end of the seventeenth century, neither Latin nor Greek played any part in moulding the mind of any class of Russian society. If we keep in mind that, up to the nineteenth century, familiarity with classical languages was indispensable to the pursuit of any serious study, that theology, philosophy and science were discussed only in these tongues, and that it was impossible to pretend to any culture without their knowledge, it becomes clear how deep a gulf was left between the Russians and other European nations. The linguistic isolation of the Russian people had several unexpected consequences. The first was the restricted use of the word, spoken and written, in the various manifestations of Russian culture. The Western mind, trained in the clear logical atmosphere of classical civilisation, found it most natural to use speech as the main channel of expression for emotions as well as for ideas. Russian culture, by comparison, appears almost speechless.

Although the Russia of the Middle Ages produced both secular and religious literature, with one or two exceptions it lacked originality and vigour. It was only in the nineteenth century, after making acquaintance with classical culture, that Russian literature reached a stage where it became capable of expressing the inner life and genuine thought of the nation.

Not so with other branches of art, which from the very start reached a high level. The beauty and craftsmanship of early Russian architecture is most remarkable, specially in the north (Pskov and Novgorod). There the tendency to imitate Byzantine art was less prominent than in the south, and Russia produced great and original builders almost simultaneously with the introduction of Christianity.

The profoundest revelations of Russian thought in the Middle Ages are found in the colours of the ikons, not in books. Music, architecture and painting, carving and embroidery were media more familiar than discourse and debate.[1]

Another result of the use of the Slavonic tongue was the absence of clericalism and legalism in the Russian Church. In the West, to be a clerk was to know Latin, and thereby to have access to sources of knowledge beyond the reach of the layman. In consequence, the clerical order became a class apart, superior to the laity. The clergy were the teachers of Christianity, and at the same time the exponents of Latin culture with its strong sense of law and duty; they were as much the secular as the spiritual leaders of the nation. This clericalism was entirely unknown to the Russian Church. The learning of its bishops and priests was open to every layman who could read. The clergy never formed a ruling class, and remained for the most part at the same cultural level as their

[1] See Prince E. Troubetskoy, *A Philosophy in Paint*, Moscow, 1915. An abbreviated English translation is published in *Sobornost*, the quarterly magazine of the Fellowship of St. Alban and St. Sergius, London, March, 1937, No. 9.

flock. In Russia it was the "saint" and not the "priest" who was the leader of the Church. This characteristic gave greater scope for spontaneity and for the prophetic element within the Church, but tended towards the undervaluation of discipline and obedience.

Thus, while the Western Church was engaged in the pursuit of learning, and showed great interest in the legal and institutional aspects of Church life, the Christians of Russia were primarily concerned with the worship of God and inner perfection. It is noteworthy that in Russia the most popular translations from the Greek Fathers were the works dealing with asceticism and conduct. Speculative theology made little appeal to the people, but in the longing for holiness, in the search for the Christian answer to the problems of daily life, in the sense of beauty in worship, the Russian Church was able to make a distinct contribution to the Christian world. The warmth and artistic perfection of the Church services was directly due to the use of Slavonic, which enabled the creative genius of the Russian nation to express itself fully through that particular channel.

Another consequence of the use of Slavonic was that, in translation, some of the most familiar Christian terms received an unusual interpretation. It will probably never be certain whether Cyril and Methodius or some of their disciples were responsible for the vocabulary of the Slavonic Bible. In either case, we can but marvel at the boldness and inspiration of those who accomplished this version. The translators acted more as prophets than as scholars; they were not afraid to replace the literal rendering of the Greek words by terms which seemed to them better to express the essence. Such, for example, was the translation of the words "martyrdom," "priesthood," "baptism," "orthodoxy," "catholicity." "To be baptised" becomes in Slavonic no longer "to be immersed," but "to take the Cross," to accept one's cross of suffering and renunciation, and to achieve through it regeneration and resurrection; all Christians were therefore "cross-bearing people." The word "orthodoxy" was translated by "right Glory," the Orthodox Church being that which glorified God aright. "Catholicity" was rendered by *sobornost*, a word which cannot be adequately translated into any Western language. It means gathering, collectivity, integrity; it denotes oneness, but without uniformity or loss of individuality. The "Catholic Church," as *Sobornaia Tserkov*, appears as the college, or, better, the congregation of the Lord: a fully Biblical conception.

Thus Russian Christianity has from the very beginning possessed several characteristics which distinguished it from the rest of the Catholic Church. Its Bible and its Creed were those of the other Christians, its worship and ecclesiastical discipline were an exact copy of the Byzantine pattern, but the understanding of these universal formulæ was an individual Russian one.

Such were the peculiar circumstances of the Christianisation of the Russian people. They received willingly their new religion, for they themselves invited the missionaries to come and baptise them. This peaceful penetration of Christianity explains the ease and spontaneity of the Russian approach to the Church. There was no break, no struggle, and though this facilitated the survival of pagan traditions among them, yet, on the other hand, it made Christianity the religion of the entire nation, not merely of the ruling and better-educated classes, as has often been the case in other countries. The Russians soon lost any feeling that the Church had been brought into their life from outside; it became a part of their national existence, and its further development followed lines peculiar to the Russian mind.

Prince Vladimir and the elders of the nation, by their deliberate choice of Byzantine Christianity, sealed the fate of the Russian people. They prepared that unique setting in which the drama of this culture evolved throughout the succeeding centuries.

If Vladimir had accepted the Latin Tradition, Russia would have been the most eastern outpost of Europe; if he had joined the brotherhood of Islam, Russia would have become the western wing of the Oriental world, but, by choosing Eastern Orthodoxy he cut Russia off from both her neighbours and thus provoked their lasting hostility.

The history of the Russian culture has been marked by several abrupt changes. Its first, Kiev, period was characterised by intercourse with western, southern and eastern neighbours. The country had many prosperous self-governing cities and was divided into a number of independent principalities linked together by the family ties of the ruling princes, who all belonged to the same House of Rurik (862–1598).

The finest representative of the Kiev culture was Prince Vladimir Monomakh (d. 1125), one of the most successful political and military leaders of that period. He is the author of an important literary monument, *The Charge to My Children*, which enjoyed great popularity among the Russian people for several centuries to come. It is a piece of autobiography combined with an advice addressed to Russian princes how to discharge their duties. Vladimir describes in it the ideal type of a Christian ruler, laying special emphasis on his moral integrity. He repudiates the lawfulness of capital punishment in a country which calls itself Christian, and reveals an enlightened and profoundly humane outlook.

He was a man of rare nobility and culture, well versed in the knowledge of European languages, and a living example of the height to which Russia ascended so quickly after her conversion to Christianity.

The Kiev period was brought to a catastrophic end by the onslaught of the Mongolian invasion (1237–42), which for centuries cut off Russia from the rest of Europe. The Tartars struck so hard that only two cities of northern Russia, Novgorod and Pskov, remained undestroyed. The country was completely ruined, its people were crushed down, and for two hundred years had to endure the horrors and humiliation of the Tartar yoke. Russia's liberation in the fifteenth century was the result of the political unification of the north-eastern provinces, under the leadership of the Moscow princes. It was a slow and painful process, for the Russians, used to the independence and self-government of pre-Tartar days, only gradually came to realise that their chance of survival depended on a new form of government, as highly centralised as that of their Oriental masters. The Russia of Moscow (fourteenth–seventeenth centuries) was a different country from the Russia of Kiev (ninth–thirteenth centuries). She was no longer a younger daughter of the Byzantine Empire, eager to learn from her great tutor; she considered herself the centre of a new civilisation, Christian by faith, but Asiatic in policy and manners.

The Russia of Moscow replaced in Northern Europe and Asia the Mongolian Empire, and by the middle of the seventeenth century her boundaries had reached the shores of the Pacific. Her culture was vigorous and fresh and was the expression of her people's belief in their special mission.

Every culture needs for its growth an inspiring ideal, an ultimate goal, accepted by its people. The Russians built their Moscow Tsardom round their belief that their capital was the third and the last Rome. This conviction was born in their minds in the fifteenth century, a period which was a turning point in the history both of East and West alike.

The collapse of Constantinople in 1453 was for Orthodox Christians a blow as bitter as the fall of Rome in the fifth century had been for Western Christendom. The Church and the Empire were believed to be both instituted by God and equally indispensable for the orderly life and salvation of Christians. When the news spread that the Emperor and the Patriarch had perished in the defence of their great city, there was all over the East a widespread fear that the end of the world was nigh. But the years went by and some other explanation of the catastrophe was called for and found, in the theory that the Empire had not been destroyed: its centre was simply transferred to the north, to distant and hitherto undistinguished Moscow.

The marriage, in 1472, of Ivan III, Grand Prince of Moscow, to Sophia Paleologos, the niece of the last Byzantine Emperor, Constantine XIII, Ivan's repudiation in 1480 of the Tartar yoke, and assumption of the title of Tsar, or Autocrat, with the double-headed eagle as his device, combined to suggest the revival of the Empire in the north. The Russians attached supreme importance to the preservation of a link of succession from Constantinople to Moscow, for it brought their new capital under the Biblical promises and blessings. Justification for belief in the special calling of Moscow was sought in the Book of the prophet Daniel (ii. 27–49, vii. 1–28, ix. 24–27), which described kingdoms as raised to pre-eminence and cast down one after another by the same Divine power. The commonly accepted interpretation of the prophetic text asserted that the two most decisive events of world history, the First and the Second Coming of the Messiah, would both take place during the ascendancy of the fourth great Empire, that of Rome. Rome was therefore truly an eternal city; but this did not mean that the power belonging to her was confined to a single spot. The Incarnation incorporated all nations of the world into the New Covenant, and made both Church and Empire truly universal. Thus the sacred centre of Christendom could be removed from Rome to Constantinople, when the former city succumbed to pride, and thence it was transferred once more, this time to the north, to Moscow.

Such an interpretation of history linked Russia with the ancient realms of Babylon, Persia, Alexandria, Rome and Constantinople. It shrouded the destiny of the young nation with the mysterious aura of Divine election. It made the Tsar of Moscow no mere local ruler, but an œcumenical sovereign, the protector of all true Christians. These prophecies seemed to summon the Russian nation to the building of a great empire, and the liberation of the oppressed Orthodox of the East.

In the first part of the sixteenth century, an elder of one of the monasteries in Pskov, a monk called Philotheus, formulated this widely held conviction. He wrote to the Moscow Prince: "The Church of old Rome fell for its heresy; the gates of the second Rome, Constantinople, were hewn down by the axes of the infidel Turks; but the Church of Moscow, the Church of the new Rome, shines brighter than the sun in the whole universe. Know, then, pious Prince, that all the realms which hold fast to the Orthodox Christian faith are now gathered together in thy dominion. Thou art the one universal Sovereign of all Christian folk; thou shouldest hold the reins in awe of God; fear Him who hath committed them to thee. Two Romes are fallen, but the third stands fast; a fourth there cannot be. Thy Christian kingdom shall not be given to another."

In these words, a Russian scholar of the sixteenth century prophetically defined his nation's place among other states, and offered an interpretation of those momentous events which had suddenly transformed his defeated country into a great Empire. The Russians experienced in these decisive years a genuine sense of resurrection. After a long period of suffering and despair, they were brought to freedom and power.

They came back to life, but the world which met them was very different from that which they had left two hundred years before. Gone were the friendly relations with their western neighbours, the lively trade with foreign countries, the self-governing and prosperous cities, and, above all, the great Byzantine Empire. Russia stood now alone in a hostile world, surrounded by Western heretics, and infidel Mahometans, with no other friend or protector but Almighty God, who had raised her from death, and revealed to her her new and awe-inspiring mission to be the guardian of Orthodox faith and worship till His Second Coming.

A number of books, partly historical, partly legendary, were produced at that time explaining to learned and simple the connection between the ancient Empire of the East and the young Tsardom of Moscow. One of the most popular stories related how the insignia of Nebuchadnezzar were discovered amidst the ruins of Babylon and solemnly brought to Constantinople. Eventually these symbols of supreme earthly power were transferred to Russsia. Thus the Moscow sovereigns claimed that their crown, which they had received from Byzantium, was even more ancient than the Eastern Empire, for it belonged originally to the great Biblical despot.

Under cover of these legendary stories, the Russians expressed their conviction that their nation was called to play the part assigned to the older monarchies of being a meeting place for the culture of East and West. Babylon, Persia, Alexandria, Rome, and then Constantinople, had all performed the same function on an ever-expanding scale—it was, to make possible the collaboration of different nations and races, incorporated into one political order.

The destruction of Byzantium by the Turks had threatened to end this work. The Mahometan civilisation, having paralysed the cultural activities of the Christians, imposed an artificial immobility upon the conquered countries and built a wall between the East and the West. But meanwhile, in the far North, in Moscow, unknown to the rest of Europe, the process of cultural co-operation was resumed, at first on a small scale, but gradually widening in its scope and purpose till Russia became a great Empire, a new link between Asia and Europe.

At the time when Philotheus wrote his epistles, Moscow was still the capital of a small principality surrounded by strong and hostile neighbours; but twenty-five years after his death her people crossed the Volga and opened the door towards the East. A hundred years later, they reached the shores of the Pacific Ocean, and in two hundred years the Russian Empire spread from the Baltic Sea to China, and from the Black Sea to Archangel.

Moscow was indeed called to continue the work of her great Imperial predecessors, and keep together the Eastern and Western elements of civilisation. Her approach to this difficult task was fresh and daring; yet the Russians had no intention of being innovators. They were trying to copy Rome and Constantinople, but they knew so little about the pattern they sought to imitate, the circumstances of their life were so different, that they became, against their will, the authors of an original culture. They built their new State, not on the site of venerable ruins, but on virgin soil not yet touched by civilisation, and they looked on the world with eyes which had never seen the great monuments of the awe-inspiring past. The Russians created their culture outside the ancient classical world, but on a pattern designed by the religious and artistic genius of the Greek and Semitic peoples. This geographical isolation of

Russian culture had far-reaching implications. The boundaries of the *Pax Romana* are more than merely the political and military frontiers of the past. Western European civilisation is still based on the territories which once formed the body of the Empire. Even such countries as modern Germany bear the lasting imprint of the Roman frontier. The Germany of the Imperial outposts, after sixteen hundred years, is still a different country from the Germany which has never seen the triumphant Roman eagles. They differ in religion and in culture, and this in spite of the fact that they are both parts of the same state, and have experienced together for centuries the influence of the same Western Christian tradition.

Russia has never been touched by the Roman Empire; geographically and spiritually, she had no direct link with the Latin world. Her isolation was completed by the hostility of Western Christians, which led the Russians to bar the doors of their hearts and minds to all currents of thought coming direct from the West. Of the four main streams of European traditions, Roman, Teutonic, Greek and Judæo-Christian, only the two last have flowed freely in Russia, but even they entered by a special channel, that of worship, and therefore took on an original form.

Russia has never been attracted by, or yielded to, the majestic tradition of the old Rome, and has met it only as a hostile force to be resisted at whatever cost. The sense of ordered discipline and responsibility, the ideal of unity based upon authority which the Eternal City bequeathed to the Western Church, to save Europe in the Dark Ages, has remained wholly unknown to her.

Again, Russia has never met, except as foes, the vigorous Teutonic peoples whose resistance to the Roman pattern explains so much of Europe's troubled history.

The only channel of Western influence which remained open was the devious route of the Byzantine Empire, with its civil and ecclesiastical legislation based on Roman law. But even this contact with the Latin mind failed to impress the Russians of Moscow, for they never properly grasped the working of the administrative side of the Byzantine Church. The Russians faithfully adhered to the three-fold ministry, and considered the canons of the ancient Councils as binding, but the position of bishops and priests in Russia was different from that which they held in the Roman Empire. Russian diocesan organisation and ecclesiastical synods looked highly irregular, judged by the standards of the Œcumenical Church.

Thus the whole idea of Roman law, of the discipline and sub-ordination, never reached the Moscow Tsardom and failed to affect the order which grew up there.

Russia remained likewise without the stimulus of Greek philosophy and dialectic. In this case the gulf between Greece and Russia was one, not of suspicion and hostility, but of geographical distance and, above all, of language. The Greeks treated the Russians, from the time of their conversion, as friendly barbarians. They made no effort to introduce to them the fullness of their cultural inheritance, and the Russians of the Kiev period, in a manner typical of adolescents, picked up and enjoyed those fruits of the Byzantine interpretation of Christianity which made the strongest appeal to them. Greece had two great achievements, her art and her logical thought. Young Russia eagerly absorbed the first and let the other go.

When, after the trials of the Tartar invasion, the Russians reached a more mature stage of development, it was too late for them to gain a more balanced view of the Greek outlook. Byzantium by that time was tottering to its fall, while the policy of concessions to the Latin West pursued by its leaders alienated the Russians, who therefore missed the opportunity for learning.

The Russians found themselves in circumstances never repeated in Europe. They were able to create their own culture on a Christian basis, outside the boundaries of classical civilisation, and they re-mained uninfluenced by Imperial Rome. The vast spaces of their own country, the talents of its people, and their firm belief in their special calling provided the Russians with the necessary strength and confidence for their ambitious enterprise of building a Christian realm which should surpass both Rome and Constantinople in its faithfulness to Christ and its zeal to apply His precepts to daily life.

The Russia of Moscow had many shortcomings; but there is no doubt that her people had a genuine conviction of the reality of her mission, and that they produced a social order which was an integral embodiment of their religious outlook.

Of this outlook the greatest representative was St. Sergius of Radonezh (1314–92), the founder and Abbot of the famous Monastery of the Holy Trinity. He stands in the very centre of Russian life. All the diverse movements of Russian thought, all the opposing tendencies of Russian mentality, converge in him,

C

find in him their solution and balance. From St. Sergius more than from anybody else, the Russian people caught their traditional ideal of unity in freedom, *sobornost*. This ideal he displayed as grounded in the true meaning of the Christian belief in the Holy Trinity.[1] His contemporary biographer expressed this conviction when he wrote that "St. Sergius built the Church of the Holy Trinity as a mirror for his community, that through contemplating the Divine Unity they might overcome the hateful divisions of this world."

St. Sergius was a living embodiment of the Trinitarian vision of life; those who came in contact with him could learn how to live in harmony and concord. His numerous disciples represented social relations of a new type, based on faith in God and mutual trust between men.

The belief that the Russians are one big family and the realisation that this unity depends neither on the compulsion exercised by the ruler nor on the legal system imposed upon them, but rests on their willing obedience to the same rhythm of life, dates from his time. He was the first to demonstrate that people could act as one body on the strength of their moral solidarity, and he therefore is the true founder of the cultural order known by the name of Orthodox Russia.

He was not, however, responsible for the political system which was gradually built up by the Moscow princes. His teaching was more authentically Christian, and his vision of national unity more free, and all-embracing, than that which appealed to the Russian autocrats. He is therefore a link between two distinct Russias; the one which became a great Empire, the successor of the Mongols, and the other the Russia of the saints, philosophers and poets, who laboured and prayed for the establishment in their land of a genuine Christian order, and whose ideal, in spite of all failures and disappointments, has remained the guiding light in the life of the Russian people.

The personalities of St. Sergius and his numerous followers were formed under the influence of the same all-powerful factor. The whole Russian life was fed by the same source of knowledge and inspiration, the only one which, in the Middle Ages, the Russians possessed: this was the liturgical services of the Orthodox Church,

[1] See N. Zernov, *St. Sergius: Builder of Russia*, S.P.C.K., 1939.

especially the Holy Eucharist. The superb beauty of Byzantine worship was, according to the chronicle, the chief reason for the Russian preference for the Eastern tradition to the Latin. This predilection remained constant throughout the history of the nation. Lacking legal training, inarticulate in speech, backward in science, the Russians became masters in the conduct of worship, and their entire culture was built around the celebration of the Divine Offices. The parish church was for the Russians their school, their concert-room, their picture gallery—all that the nation possessed which was creative in thought or art found its expression in the worship of the Church. The Eastern Orthodox Eucharist is a piece of perfectly dramatised action, which only the genius of the Greeks could ever devise. It contains a symbolic representation of the whole story of the Incarnation. The priest manifests the figure of Christ; the deacon, accompanied by the choir, comments on His actions; whilst the congregation, moved by faith and love for its Saviour, lives through all the stages of His Life. It hears the preaching of His Gospel; it laments His Suffering and Death; and rejoices at the sight of His Resurrection—this victory of love over the powers of evil and death.

The most remarkable feature of this service is its corporate nature. The priest is little heard and often remains unseen behind the solid screen. It is not he who celebrates for the laity as is the case in the West. In the East the Eucharist is conducted by the joint action of priest, deacon, choir and people, who all have their well-defined parts to play and are equally indispensable to the service. The rite is both solemn and homely; all its main movements are fixed, and yet its performance is spontaneous and free. The symbolism is so well-balanced that it is both profound and simple, and can be understood by learned and unlearned alike.

When Russia was cut off by the Tartars from the rest of the Christian world, when her cities and towns were destroyed, the only link with the past was the traditional setting of the liturgical offices, and the Russians made full use of their rich content. Men, women and children[1] acted for generations in this unique religious drama, and derived from it a Christian philosophy of life which permeated their entire existence. The outlook which was contained in the services implied belief in man's unique value, and in his freedom. For though made of dust, infected by sin, and condemned to pain and sorrow, he was so treasured by the Creator

[1] Russian children are confirmed when they are baptised and so enjoy the status of communicants from the beginning of their lives.

that God Himself became Man. A Russian knew that his present state of degradation was only temporary, that he was created in the image of God, and that he was called to take an active part in the transfiguration and redemption of the universe. The purpose of human life was conceived as approximation to the Divine prototype. The Russian language powerfully expresses this conviction; people who show the example of a better and purer life are called *prepodobnye*, which, literally, means "most like." In other words, holy men and women are those who approach nearest to the original picture of man. On the contrary, every form of ugliness, violence and disorder is branded by the word *besobrazie*, "that which lost its image," or unseemliness. The Russians believed that life on earth was a test, wherein everyone could choose either to live a selfish existence, which led to divisions and strifes, or to become a member of a Christian family, united in love and freedom. The Holy Spirit was the source of unity among people; where He was, there concord, peace and perfect freedom reigned. Outside His realm men were haunted by fear and hatred.

The greatest achievements of Russian culture were a deep understanding of man and the longing for a righteous social order. The Russians were neither naïve nor sentimental; they were equally free from rosy optimism and gloomy despair.

On every Sunday and feast-day the Russians, gathered in their parish churches, stood in front of the screen on which the images of the Saints were painted; those transfigured and glorified figures represented members of past generations from all nations and races who had passed through hard trials and temptations of flesh and spirit, and had been victorious.

The road to the ultimate goal was the same for every Christian: it was summarised for the Russians in the Beatitudes. The Western social and political order has been built on the idea of law; the Ten Commandments, the Roman ideal of justice and the notion of privilege were the three solid pillars which supported the imposing edifice of European civilisation. But the Russians were brought up in the spirit of the Sermon on the Mount. They listened for centuries, at every Eucharist, to the words of this most challenging, most paradoxical definition of the purpose of human life, and of the means of achieving perfection. A Russian might be a good man or a bad man, he might try to apply its teaching to his life, or act contrary to its precepts, but he had no doubt that this was the final revelation of truth, and that there was no other path to bring man to life and happiness. The Russians often failed to show those virtues which were particularly valued by Western Christians, but their great moral achievements were their readiness to forgive offenders, their genuine humility and charity, and, above all, their understanding of the mutual responsibility of all. They believed in God's mercy for sinners, they trusted in man's ability to distinguish between good and evil, and considered that healthy social life was the condition of moral growth for an individual. They were convinced that the ideal of the Christian family with its atmosphere of mutual help, love and freedom was God's intended pattern for the Christian social order, and felt confident that, in spite of human frailty and sin, it was a realisable plan. The Russians of Moscow had no confidence in human justice, but firmly trusted in Divine guidance, and knew that the Holy Spirit, the only source of life and truth, spoke through the free and unanimous voice of the assembled people. It did not matter whether they had or had not political rights and economic freedom; they all as Christians could hear the voice of God and act according to His commandment.

This philosophy of life explains why the Russian peasants even during their serfdom were able to preserve their sense of human dignity, and to keep intact the tradition of self-government in their rural communities in spite of centuries of oppression and social degradation. It explains, too, why, although the political system of Moscow was despotic, the people were yet free, and had a genuine feeling that all Russians were equal to one another. The peculiar set of historical circumstances which had created the arbitrary rule of the Tsars with its power to dispose of the lives and property of any of their subjects had not obliterated the knowledge that these same subjects, as bearers of the Divine image, were all members of one Christian family. Any Russian, including the highest officers of State, might prostrate himself before his sovereign, but the same Tsar was still a fellow sinner, as much in need of God's mercy as was the poorest beggar of his realm. In the present world the Tsar was omnipotent; but there was another world where values were reversed, where the powerful and privileged had to yield place of honour to the poor and the afflicted, for to these, Gospel blessings were promised and the bliss of communion with God was reserved.

Faith in the goodness of God's created world, and in the ultimate victory of righteousness over selfishness and discord, made the

culture of Moscow, in spite of all its limitations, capable of up-
lifting the life of individuals as well as of the whole nation. The
Russians were crude and undisciplined, and lacked refinement;
they often succumbed to their passions and sins, and suffered
frequently from all forms of abuse of power; cruelty and vice
mutilated the life of millions, but all this was unable to quench their
longing for holiness, and to destroy their firm belief that man
could never be satisfied and happy except when he followed the
Sermon on the Mount.

Russian art of that period provides a valuable material for the
study of the outlook of Moscow people. It was predominantly
religious, its purpose was to serve the entire community, and it
was understood and appreciated, not by a small group of connois-
seurs alone, but by the generality of people. Only those arts
flourished which were incorporated into Church worship. Sculp-
ture and instrumental music, barred from the decoration and
services of the Eastern Church, were practically unknown in
Russia, but singing, painting and architecture were fully developed
and appreciated.

Painting was known to the Russians chiefly in the two forms of
mural frescoes, which decorated both the outside walls and the
interiors of the churches, and of portable ikons. Their subjects
were either figures of the Saints or scenes from the Old and New
Testaments, or symbolic representations of the cardinal doctrines
of Christianity.

The Russians learned the art of painting from Byzantine masters,
and through this channel they became acquainted with the achievements of the Hellenistic world. Cut off from a knowledge of Greek
philosophy and poetry, they were yet at home in the realm of its
pictorial art. They were also influenced by Oriental artists, especially
by the fine craftsmanship of the Persian miniaturists. The ikons
were for the Russians an artistic symbol of the Christian victory
over the powers of sin, chaos and destruction. The ikons were
not merely painted wood; they were the dynamic manifestations
of a redeemed and harmonised world, constant reminders of its
glory and beauty. They were a source of hope, consolation and
inspiration to Christians amidst the suffering and disappointments
of their earthly life. Every parish church was richly adorned with
frescoes and ikons, every house had a so-called "red corner," where

the ikons were placed and where occasional Church services and family prayers were said. In peace and danger, at home or on a journey, in the happiest hours of his life and at the point of death a Russian wanted to see an ikon, to touch it, to kiss it and to be comforted by it. Some of these ikons acquired nation-wide fame; miracles of healing were connected with them; they accompanied the army in the field, and the safety and protection of the country were entrusted to their charge.

The importance attributed to the ikons seems unintelligible, even shocking, to foreign observers of Russian life. Charges of gross superstition, of idolatry, and confusion between the inanimate picture and the person represented by it have often been made against the Russians. These attacks, however, arise from a misunderstanding of the outlook of the Russian Christians. For them matter and spirit were manifestations of the same reality, completing and fulfilling each other. The opposition between them, the apparent grossness of matter, they treated as a false impression created by sin, which has distorted both the proper function of the physical elements and man's control over them. Sin, however, could not completely obliterate the original harmony between man and the rest of creation. The Church exercised its regenerating influence on matter and spirit alike, and restored them to their beauty, health and unity. Art was treated as one of the means at the disposal of redeemed mankind to extend the realm of the Holy Spirit, and to accelerate the process of transfiguration of both the material world and the human race. Seen from this point of view, the colours and lines of an ikon were not only a reflection of the celestial glory, but the actual focus of the operation of the Holy Spirit. Their matter was restored to harmony and became once more a vehicle of the Spirit, freely and spontaneously answering to His call. The veneration of the ikons by the Russians was therefore an application of that same belief in the Incarnation which, as underlying the Catholic *cultus* of the Eucharistic Sacrament, has been the doctrine so fundamental to the development of Western thought and social action.

From a technical point of view, Russian religious painting stood on a high level. Its chief achievements were perfection in colour and rhythm in composition. It made no attempt to imitate Nature; its purpose was to demonstrate that men, animals and plants and the whole cosmos, can be redeemed from their present state of degradation, and are capable of becoming obedient to the Holy Spirit. The sacred pictures were not actual portraits of the Saints, they were anticipations of their celestial glory. Although the resemblance to the model was as far as possible preserved, the artist laid the main stress, not on the likeness, but on the victory of the new creation in the saint over his old and sinful self.

The expression of the saints depicted was severe and ascetic, the movements of their bodies were restrained, but the colours of their robes were shining, and their faces turned towards the new world. Its hope and joy were reflected in their eyes, and the contrast between the immobility of their bodies and the intense liveliness of their eyes emphasised the complete control of their mind over their flesh. The Muscovite artists were convinced that this was the only road which could bring the cosmos and mankind, its spokesman, out of its present captivity into harmony and freedom. Their beliefs found further expression in the architecture of the Russian churches.

Most Russian churches were built with a domed roof, which embodied the idea of the heavenly sphere. It represented the universe created by a perfect Architect and ruled by an omnipotent Master. But outside this dome there was another, this time the real vault of heaven, and this reminded Christians that the earth has not yet attained its glory, and is only aspiring to it. The task of the Church was to assist and direct this process, for its realisation required further effort and further ascent. In order to express this, the church dome on the outside took another form, that of a tapering flame. The brightly coloured, onion-shaped cupola was the earth itself, wrapped in prayer, reaching up to the triumphant, glittering Cross, the symbol of the victory of life over death. On the flat plains of Russia its innumerable churches, with their shining colours and strange shapes, looked like fragments of another celestial world scattered over the country as a token of the coming transfiguration of men and of earth itself.

The Russian architects, armed with a profound sense of conviction and practical skill, proclaimed their belief in the new redeemed world which will one day appear in its full glory and beauty, not out of nothing, but from the material which has been used for the building up of the present one. With prophetic eyes, they saw signs that this transformation was already begun, in spite of all the disharmony and shortcomings of the universe as it was known to them. The grimmer the struggle, the more severe and unfriendly Nature, the stronger was their faith in the ultimate victory of good. It is significant that the largest number of churches dedicated to the Feast of the Transfiguration is found in the inhospitable region of the extreme north, where men had to use all their energy and perseverance to survive in the Arctic cold.

Besides painting and architecture, the Russians used another art for the expression of their outlook, an art which has no proper name in Western languages, but was the most important manifestation of Russian culture. In Russian this is described under the name of *Bytovoe Blagochestie*. Its literal translation would be "the piety of daily life," but the "ritual art of living" probably conveys more nearly its true meaning. It was an attempt on the part of the whole nation to find a sacred pattern for its daily life, to incorporate all events and actions, big and small, private and public, in corporate worship. It was also the most powerful link which kept the Russians together. The Moscow Tsardom was based neither on a national nor a legal conception of the State. It was essentially the private domain of the Moscow Prince, inhabited by a great variety of races and nations; the relations between the Sovereign and his subjects were never clearly defined. Yet the Russians lived in organic unity with one another, for the majority of them voluntarily followed the same rhythm of life. Rich and poor, freemen and serfs, the Tsar and the lowest beggar, carefully and devoutly observed the same customs, fasted on some days and feasted on others together. They all attended the same service, loved the same music, enjoyed the same architecture and painting, for they all believed in the same truth.

The ritual art of living was expressed in solemn nation-wide festivals, in which the Tsar, clergy and people took part, but its manifestations were no less devoutly observed in every Russian home. It controlled the behaviour of the individual as much as did all the official functions of Church and State.

The birth of a child, marriages or funerals, all the happy and unhappy events of human life, the visit of a guest, the start of a journey, all were the occasions for some rite. Food, clothing, manners, meals, the way they greeted each other and expressed their sorrows or joy, all were made part of the great dramatic theme, of which the source of inspiration was the story of the Incarnation.

On the most solemn occasions, the Tsar, as the head of the family, performed the role of the "man," "the first Adam," the crown of creation, endowed with the power of intimate communion with God, and yet capable of sinking lower than any of the brutes. The Patriarch, as the high priest, represented the "Saviour of the World," the "second Adam," who took the form of a slave and as a humble, suffering servant redeemed the first Adam from his state of degradation, and showed him the way to Heaven. The lay people, men, women, and children, played the same role as the Tsars, while clergy formed the chorus of the Patriarch. The whole nation as one body enacted all the main stages of the Redemption. It was a living drama to which fresh scenes were added yearly by the canonisation of new saints and by the institution of new festivals.

The idea of such a divine drama was borrowed by the Russians from the Byzantine Empire, but they introduced so many novel elements into it that they transformed it into their own original creation. The main Russian achievement was to make the rhythm of the movement so perfect that the whole nation could act as one body in which every individual felt himself at unity with the others and yet spontaneous and free. This was the Russian ideal expressed by the word *sobornost*—the togetherness or oneness of life, unrestricted by any legal or intellectual barriers, but obeying the guidance of the Holy Spirit, and therefore enjoying unity in complete freedom.

Much has happened in Russia since the time of the Moscow Tsardom. The upper classes became secularised and Westernised, and lost their organic link with the nation; the lower classes were profoundly affected by social unrest and religious dissent, and yet, in spite of all these disintegrating influences, up to the very eve of the Communist Revolution the Russians still continued to act as one body on the occasions of great Church and national festivals, and on the days of family feasts. But, impressive as they were, these customs were only the poor remnants of their past glory, the climax of which had been reached three hundred years before.

As an example of the survival of this art, in the twentieth century, the Easter Service in Moscow might be quoted. On that night few people could remain in their homes. The entire population flocked to churches and filled the courtyards and streets around them. A specially large crowd would be gathered in the Kremlin. In silence, the crowds awaited the coming of midnight, signalled by the first stroke sounded on the biggest bell in Russia, in the belfry of Ivan the Great. There was an interval of acute tension, then the second stroke resounded, filling the air with its magnificent sound, and at once the innumerable bells of Moscow burst out in a frenzy of triumphant clamour. Thousands of men and boys had been waiting this moment for hours in every belfry. Ivan the Great announced the Resurrection, and all the other bells responded to it. The number of churches which joined in this chorus swelled every moment, gradually widening the circle round the Kremlin till, first, the churches in the suburbs, then those in the towns and villages round, were caught in the mighty current of sound. No other country has ever known such hilarious, intoxicating bell-ringing as that of Moscow on Easter night. The air seemed turned to sound; not man alone but Nature itself seemed to be proclaiming the truth of the Resurrection on that night.

At that moment all Russians were once more united: Christians and agnostics, good and bad, all were one body, conscious of their common manhood, redeemed and released by the power that raised Christ from the dead. The Kremlin, at the very heart of the nation, was the centre of the Easter night's drama, but every Russian village, every parish church, had its share in this action: everywhere the same ceremonies were performed, the same joyous tunes were sung, the same emotions were experienced.

The Easter night service was so impressive because it was not mere ecclesiastical ceremony followed by a faithful few; it was an action in which the entire nation took a prominent part.

The ritual art of living is widespread among most Asiatic peoples. China, India, and Japan have developed it, each in their own way, but Russia was the only Christian country in which it reached a high level of perfection, and retained it till the twentieth century. It has so deeply influenced all spheres of Russian life that, in spite of the anti-religious propaganda launched by the Communists, the unity of the Russian folk still depends more on customary style of living than on any other factor.

Such were some of the manifestations of Russian culture. Its character was also reflected in the various social and political achievements of the Moscow Tsardom, such as the wide extension of self-government, not only to the village and town communities, but sometimes to entire provinces. In the fifteenth and sixteenth centuries many regions had only elected officials. The same spirit animated the work of the consultative National Assemblies, which played an important part in the course of the sixteenth and seventeenth centuries. These organs of public opinion represented all classes, and they saved the country from the anarchy of the "Time of Troubles" (1598–1613), by electing the new dynasty of the Romanovs, and assisting them in their task of national reconstruction. The same determination of the nation to live in unity and freedom was shown in the independent communities of the Cossacks, one of the most original and successful of Russian social experiments.

Russian life was permeated from top to bottom by the family idea. It was expressed through the universal custom of addressing people only by their Christian names; by the open hospitality of Russian homes, where shelter and food were offered free to strangers; by the meetings of the rural community, the *Mir*, at which both the general and the domestic problems were discussed; by the *Skhod*, or popular assemblies of the freedom-loving Cossacks; by the moral authority of the National Assemblies; by the willing obedience given to the elders, *Starosta*, who managed the affairs of the *Artels*, self-governing fraternities of artisans; by the name "Father" given to the Tsars; and by the widespread conviction of the equality and mutual responsibility of all the children of the great Russian motherland.

The Russians described themselves by the name "Orthodox," and this is a custom still widely spread among the peasants. Such self-identification with the true profession of Christianity indicates that they considered religion and not nationality as the real foundation of their unity. The social organisation of the nation was far from perfection, but people lived as one body, and that gave them strength to face courageously their hardships and privations. Only those decisions were treated as binding which were made in unanimity, the power of compulsion was mistrusted; and this was yet another proof that the Russians held their ideal in all earnest, and were ready to sacrifice efficiency and material comforts for the sake of preserving it.

Remarkable as were the achievements of Muscovite culture, they were counterbalanced by no less serious defects and failures. Their root cause was the predominant influence of one particular school of thought, which gained a complete ascendancy over other traditions in the course of the sixteenth century. The shortcomings of the Moscow Tsardom were mostly due to the political victory of the Possessors over the Non-possessors. Such were the nicknames given to two opposite parties into which the movement of national and religious revival started by St. Sergius became divided in the fourteenth century. The whole country took an active interest in them, but because the monasteries were the centres of Russian culture at that time, the leadership of these conflicting tendencies fell into the hands of the monks. Two of them, St. Joseph of Volotsk (1439–1515) and St. Nil of Sorsk (1433–1508), are their best-known representatives. Both shared the conviction typical to all Russian Christians that worship is man's highest activity, and mankind can find its true unity and purpose only in the corporate glorification of the Triune Creator. Agreeing, however, on these broad principles, they disagreed on their practical implications.

St. Joseph and his followers laid their main stress on the beauty and artistic perfection of corporate worship. They conceived as their ideal of society a community engaged in never-ceasing praise of their Lord and Maker. This act of praise included all forms of human activity, charitable and artistic, the instruction of the ignorant, the patient and conscientious carrying out of one's own duties; but all these actions were only subsidiaries to the most perfect expression of man's devotion to his Creator, the orderly rendering of Divine Service. Here every detail mattered supremely, for all was prescribed by the Holy Spirit, who spoke through the sacred tradition of the Apostles and Fathers.

Because monks and nuns, free from all earthly concerns, alone could perform this important function properly, they were treated as the most important members of society. Each individual was considered a participant in the majestic, rhythmical movement, carefully planned and lovingly executed. Life was severe and ascetic, but there was nothing dreary or monotonous about it. St. Joseph was himself a great artist. He was one of the best singers of his time, and Russia has always been a country of good singers; he had a fine taste for colour and design, the vestments he wore were unsurpassed in their beauty, the churches he built were masterpieces of Russian architecture. Joseph and his school firmly believed in the unquestionable superiority of Russian culture over all others, for Russia stood ahead of others in the supreme art of worship, and was defective only in those things in which they had no interest.

Politically, they supported strong paternal autocracy, believing that it was best suited for the maintenance of their ideal—a nation living and acting as one worshipping community. The Josephians were in favour of monastic property; they had no scruples over allowing the monks to possess serfs, whose labour provided the religious with the material conditions necessary for their charitable works and for the undisturbed conduct of the services. The Possessors were good practical landlords and the monasteries controlled by them prospered. They advocated severe punishment by the State of all dissenters, and they were mistrustful of human reason and suspicious of learning.

Some of the most typical features of Russian mentality were represented by Joseph and his party, but equally characteristic of the Russian outlook were St. Nil and his followers. They too treated worship as the main purpose of human life, but for them God wanted from His creatures above all else, a faithful and loving heart which in perfect freedom should render praise and devotion to the Creator.

The Non-possessors were ascetics. They were men of contemplation. They never built big monasteries; they refused to use gold, silver and precious stones for the decoration of their churches; they even considered that organised charity for the poor was the duty of the lay people, not of the monks, who ought to have no possessions and live entirely on the fruits of their labours. The Russians are artistic, but not romantic; when they are interested in intellectual problems, they display a preference for concrete and precise studies. St. Nil was one of the representatives of this trend of Russian thought. He was not afraid to expose his belief to the test of rational investigation, and he accepted the authority of the Scriptures and tradition only after a careful examination of all the evidence available at his time.

Freedom, personal responsibility and keen concern for each individual were the keynotes of his teaching, and on this ground he and his followers were stubbornly opposed to many ideas advocated by the Possessors. St. Nil, for instance, insisted that torture and death sentences against heretics were contrary to the spirit of the Gospel, since they made it impossible for sinners to repent and to be reconciled to the Church.

It is significant that at the time when in Western Europe the persecution of heretics was universally approved, in Russia the aversion to capital punishment, already felt by the Christians of the Kiev period, was again expressed and with even stronger emphasis by a large and influential school of thought.

The Possessors and the Non-possessors were complementary

movements, both essential to the harmonious growth of Russian culture. All its most creative manifestations have contained elements taken from both of those traditions. Accordingly, the failures and distortions of Russian life have usually been due to the assertion of one of them at the expense of the other.

Unfortunately for the destiny of the country, the desire to obtain permission to divorce forced Basil III (1505–33), the Prince of Moscow, to ally himself with the party of the Possessors, who were willing to grant it to the Prince, whilst their opponents, the Non-possessors, refused this ·concession. This political intervention upset the balance between the two parties, and led to the exclusion of the Non-possessors from active participation in the building up of Moscow Tsardom in the sixteenth and seventeenth centuries, the time of its rapid expansion. Thus the Russian culture of that period bears the marks of the exclusive influence of the Possessors' mentality. It became excessively ritualistic, stagnant intellectually, and too ready to sacrifice an individual for the sake of the community. The cost of strong communal sense was paid in the evasion of personal responsibility, in the failure to breed men of moral courage, and in the rarity of outstanding personalities. Any man who wanted to think for himself was in danger of departing from the traditional pattern, and therefore was suspected and discouraged by others. Everyone who dared to raise his voice in protest against accepted custom was ostracised. Cruelty and crime, if committed, not by the individual, but by the collective body, were excused. The Tsars, as the heads of the community, were treated, in Oriental fashion, as persons responsible only to God for their conduct; their actions were not judged by the moral standards of the ordinary man. The centuries of the Tartar yoke had left a deep trace on Russian mentality. They encouraged the growth of passive resignation before the supreme power, and readiness to submit unconditionally to the rule of the autocrat. It was not by chance that Russian legend crowned the Moscow Tsars with the Insignia of the Babylonian despots. Russia was not only a Christian family; she was also an Oriental monarchy which required from its people a blind obedience to the sovereign. Russia was deplorably lacking in legal notions. Her people had little sense of their rights and obligations; their adherence to the family ideal exposed them to the danger of domestic tyranny and arbitrary oppression. Her people aspired to holiness, but were inclined to disregard more prosaic but nevertheless all-important virtues of honesty, sobriety and truthfulness. Their ideals were high and inspiring, but when they failed to reach them, they had nothing else to sustain them, and they sank low in their moral and physical degradation. These shortcomings led to the clumsiness of the administration, the inferiority of the army organisation, the pitiful neglect of the proper development of industry, and a low standard of production. But the main social defect was the gradual reduction of the free peasants to serfdom. The bitter resentment which serfdom bred sapped the vitality of national life.

Serfdom was imposed upon the Russians by their military and technical backwardness. The long, unprotected frontier, out of all proportion to the scattered population, constantly menaced by hostile neighbours, required extraordinary measures of defence. These included a permanent universal conscription of the entire population. A section of it, "the serving gentry," provided the country with militia, ready at the shortest notice to take up arms in defence of the land. The rest were obliged to supply these gentry with their living by working on their land. At first these lands were given, in temporary possession only, to the serving gentry in payment of their military duties, but towards the end of the sixteenth century many of the estates began to be treated as private property, and the peasants who inhabited them as the serfs of their owners.

Serfdom in Russia arose as a temporary measure, as an abuse caused by confused political thinking, but its disastrous results were far-reaching. They distorted the whole of Russian life. Through serfdom, National Assemblies, so prominent in the sixteenth and the first part of the seventeenth century, fell into decay. Provincial self-government was abandoned. The mass rebellions of the embittered peasants called forth drastic measures of suppression, which encouraged the growth of the arbitrary and oppressive rule of the central government. Russia, by the adoption of serfdom, failed to reach her original objective of establishing a family relation among her people, but this sacrifice of freedom failed to secure for the nation immunity from foreign aggression. By the end of the seventeenth century Russia became painfully aware of her inferiority in all technical and military matters. All her efforts to regain free access to the Black and the Baltic Seas, lost during the time of the Tartar invasion, and so vital for the restoration of her contacts with other parts of the world, ended in complete failure. This military weakness, coupled with a growing conviction that it was their duty to assist the other Eastern Christians suffering under Mahometan and Latin oppression, forced the Russian people to recognise the need of learning from the West. This was a hard and unenviable task. The Russians felt superior to other nations because in the most important sphere of life, in Christian faith and worship, they believed that they alone held, in its purity, the truth lost or perverted by the rest of Christendom.

The moral conflict created by the clash of national pride and the sense of military inferiority divided the leaders of the Russian nation. The Russian Church, which hitherto had enjoyed happy relations with the Moscow Tsardom, became the scene of intense conflict which was to rend it asunder. The Schism of the Old Believers in the middle of the seventeenth century (1653–67) was caused by the attempts of the Tsar and the Patriarch to force the Russians to give up their claims to religious superiority. This schism cut away from the main body a large group of influential Churchmen[1] and at the same time ended the alliance between the Church and State as two equal partners. This meant a breakdown of the Moscow culture, and the moral bankruptcy of the party of the Possessors which had been dominant for more than two hundred years. The need of drastic reforms became obvious, and they were executed with ruthless vigour by Peter the Great (1689–1725).

Russia was brought back into the society of European nations, her people learned technical science from the West and became an important military power. Their artistic and cultural life was enriched, and they produced great literature of the nineteenth century. Unfortunately, however, Peter the Great acted too rashly. When under his mighty blows the wall of separation was destroyed, new ideas flooded the country. The upper classes were carried away by the powerful stream of foreign life, and lost contact with their own homeland. Only those who have lived for generations under the rule of communal discipline, only those who are used to a definitely marked rhythm of corporate life, can imagine the intoxication that was felt by those Russians who followed the example of Peter the Great.

The cumbrous national dresses, the strict rules of fasting, the universal attendance at long services, and the elaborate conventions of daily life all vanished at a blow. Men could do what they liked. The Tsar was the first to set the example of complete disregard for the venerable traditions of the past. Those who imitated him went further. For Peter attacked Muscovite customs only for the sake of Western efficiency. He sought to replace the family ideal of the old Tsardom by a powerful bureaucratic and militarist

[1] For further description of this schism, see N. Zernov, *Moscow, the Third Rome*, S.P.C.K.

D

State of the European type. But most of those who obeyed his orders cared for nothing but their own pleasure; they were delighted to see the sacred traditions outraged, corporate authority challenged, and their fleshly cravings licensed. These Russians disdainfully dissociated themselves from their cultural past, began to imitate the latest movements of European thought and manners, declaring that their own nation had never been able to make any contribution to the civilisation of mankind.[1] This attitude, however, was taken only by a minority of the Russians, the bulk of the people, merchants, clergy and peasants, remained faithful to their traditional outlook, resenting and mistrusting Western ways of life. They shut their doors more closely than before, stubbornly opposing all concessions to Europe.

The St. Petersburg Empire (1701–1917) was built, therefore, on an unsure foundation. In spite of its forbidding ramparts, a deep rift was widening between the rulers and the ruled. The masses were discontented and alien institutions borrowed from the West were never accepted and properly assimilated.

The collapse of the Empire in 1917 was due to the mistakes committed by its great founder. These were aggravated by the folly of his successors, who, being mostly Germans by birth and mentality, had little knowledge of the country which they were called to govern. The danger of a revolution had been foreseen by many Russians; the problem which exercised their minds was the possibility of fusing the old culture of Moscow with the civilisation of the West. The Russia of St. Petersburg failed to achieve a satisfactory synthesis between them, and perished in so failing. Whether her fate indicates the incompatibility of the two outlooks which her leaders tried to combine, or whether other measures might have succeeded, is a problem which concerns both Russia and Europe, for their future is bound together.

There are many similarities but also many contrasts between the Russian and the Western mind, for Russian culture is a genuine mixture of the Asiatic and European traditions. Many of its characteristics are common to all Oriental races, but its emphasis on the value of personality and its social activism are typical of the

[1] Russia differs from the West in that her true culture is represented mostly by her lower classes, especially the peasants. Its essentially artistic foundation makes possible even to the illiterate a full participation in it. The upper Russian classes, however, owing to the abandoning of religion, were often most ignorant of their own cultural inheritance, and they were responsible for giving the impression to the West that the majority of their people were ignorant and uncultured, an idea widespread in Europe till the present time.

Christian outlook. Russia is a meeting-place between Europe and Asia, and there both can feel at home and contribute in equality to the growth of its civilisation.

The Russian outlook holds great possibilities, but dangers too. Russia's main weakness has always been the isolation of its people and their strong sense of self-sufficiency, which made them blind to their limitations and unwilling to learn from others. No nation can develop normally, however, without interchange of ideas with others, and the establishment of the right type of co-operation with the rest of Europe and Asia has always been the main problem of Russian life. The first man who faced realistically the question of relations between Russia and the Christian West and gave a consistent answer to it was a retired Captain of the Horse Guards, Alexei Stepanovich Khomiakov.

Chapter Two

KHOMIAKOV

Alexei Khomiakov was born on May 1st, 1804. His ancestors on both sides had belonged for generations to the landed gentry. He was brought up on the family estate and received the usual education of his class and time. His tutor was a French *émigré*, the Abbé Boivin. Under his instruction, Khomiakov was introduced to the classics of European culture. From his early youth he was perfectly at home with it. The boy showed an exceptional aptitude for languages, and could speak and write French, English or German like a native. He knew Latin, Greek and also Sanskrit so well that he even produced a Sanskrit dictionary.

On one occasion, reading a mediæval Papal Bull, he discovered an error in Latin grammar, and challenged his tutor on the doctrine of Papal infallibility, which could admit such errors in an official utterance. The boy was duly reprimanded for this attack on his tutor's religious convictions; but in this incident one can see already some of the characteristics of the future leader of the Slavophils; his gift for languages, his interest in history, and his love of argument and controversy.

There was nothing unusual in a young Russian of Khomiakov's social standing being brought up in the knowledge of European culture. The exceptional feature of his education was rather his familiarity with his own tongue and background. This was the great gift which his mother, Maria Alexeevna Kireevskaia, bestowed upon her three children.

Their father, Stepan Khomiakov, was a man of literary tastes and attractive personality, but, like many other landed gentry of his day, he took little interest in practical affairs and preferred to spend his time over cards at his club.

The family was brought by his behaviour to the verge of ruin, but the situation was saved by his wife, who took into her hands the management of their estates. She was one of those strong, masterful Russian women who have so often played a leading part in Russian life. She too had received a Western education, but, being like many

KHOMIAKOV

women strongly conservative, she had kept a truly Russian outlook and strictly adhered to the Orthodox pattern of daily life. Under her influence, her family was brought up in the atmosphere of Russian traditional piety. She was neither anti-Western nor obscurantist; she wanted her children to benefit from the best that Europe could give, but she was equally determined to teach them to love and appreciate their own culture. It was an attitude most unusual in a time of such unbounded admiration for Europe and such general contempt for the Russian past. Alexei Khomiakov, who wholeheartedly accepted his mother's outlook, accordingly remained all his life a lonely and misunderstood figure among the men of his own class and generation. The Khomiakovs spent the winter in Moscow, the summer on their estates, and all the year round observed the customs and traditions of Russian Orthodoxy; kept the fasts; went to Church; read the Fathers and the lives of the Saints and gave hospitality to strangers.

They had many friends and relations, and the children were early introduced into social life. They formed many lasting friendships, some of which, like that of the brothers Kireevski, were to have an important influence upon Alexei's life. His education followed the usual lines; when his tuition at home was over, he entered Moscow University and read mathematics. In 1822 he joined the Army, and soon obtained a commission in the Horse Guards. In those years before the Decembrist rising of 1825, the officers of the Guards stood for all that was the most advanced in the life of Russian educated society. The leading minds among them were profoundly influenced by French political and philosophical ideas, but young Khomiakov, with his Russian outlook, found himself isolated from the interests and aspirations of the St. Petersburg aristocracy. As, moreover, a military career held little attraction for him, he decided to resign his commission, and in 1824 he left Russia and spent almost two years in Paris studying painting.

In one of his letters to his family, dated from the time of his visit to France, he casually remarks that he had succeeded in keeping all the rules of the Lenten fast in spite of being in Paris. The Russian Lent is severe; it excludes for seven weeks, besides meat and fish, milk, butter and eggs, and it required a strong will and great effort for a young man to abstain to this extent in Paris of all places. Khomiakov was not exceptionally ascetic, nor even a precisian. He was simply a Russian who felt his unity with his people so deeply that it was unimaginable for him to eat, even in remote France, food which was banished from a Russian table. He lived the life of his nation, and therefore freely and willingly obeyed the rhythm of its movement.

On his return to Russia he helped his mother in the administration of the family estates. This did not last long, however. The declaration of war against Turkey (1828-9) brought him back to the army. He served with distinction, but as soon as the war was over retired to civil life once more. In 1836 he married Katerina Mikhailovna Iazykova, a sister of the well-known poet, Nikolai Iazykov. He was exceptionally happy in his marriage. His wife fully shared his convictions and gave him unfailing support in all his work. They had four sons and five daughters.

The rest of his life Khomiakov spent between Moscow and his estates; he never held any governmental post, and no academic distinctions were ever offered him. He died of cholera at the age of fifty-six on September 23rd, 1860, while treating his peasants during an epidemic.

Such was the life of the great leader of the Slavophil movement. It contained few external events of importance; its significance lay in the intellectual and spiritual combats in which he took such a prominent part.

The most striking feature of Khomiakov's personality was a rare combination of many-sided gifts and interests with an exceptional single-mindedness. It is difficult to select a sphere of life which made no appeal to him—to which he had nothing to contribute. Khomiakov was poet, artist, philologist and linguist, historian, philosopher, journalist and politician; he was a self-taught doctor, a successful landlord, a capable engineer and an inventor, an enthusiastic shot, and an original and daring theologian. With such a variety of interests and gifts, only his rare integrity kept him from wasting his life and achieving nothing.

The first impression he produced was that of energy and intellectual brilliance. There was something fascinating about him. He had a dark, almost Oriental, complexion; his family, like many among the Russian nobility, had Tartar blood. He was not tall, but looked taller than he was, with his high forehead and keen eyes. As soon as he joined any company, he became the natural centre of it.

He was gay, spirited and good-humoured. He was well known for his laughter, so wholehearted, so genuine and irresistible that it carried away both friend and foe alike, and opened to them the world of spontaneous joy that is inhabited only by the pure in heart.

Khomiakov was a born speaker; his words kindled others, and his mind worked better when he had an audience in front of him. He enjoyed argument and in controversy he was a formidable opponent, with his memory, his erudition, and his wit. He might look as though he were merely showing off, but behind the sparkling eloquence there was in him an uncompromising devotion to truth, strong faith, genuine humility and a warm heart. The same Khomiakov who could talk with authority and enthusiasm on almost any subject, whose writings discussed with the same absorbing interest theology and railways, Russian history and English hunting, was equally remarkable for the steadfastness and consistency with which he maintained all his life long the principles he had learned and embraced as a boy. His interests were manifold, his responses vivid and often unexpected, but his roots were firm and set deep in the native soil that he knew and loved as no other Russian of his generation.

All that he did, said, or wrote sprang from the same underlying experience. There was only one source of inspiration in his whole life, and that was his belief in the unique truth of Christianity. The greatest treasure for him was his membership in the Church.

Many of his friends and disciples were keen and devout Orthodox, but their attitude to the Church was different from his. Some had not been brought up as Christians, and had found their way to faith only after long struggle. Others had left the Church in their youth and come back after wandering far from the home of their spiritual birth. For both the Church was a treasure house which they had discovered. It was the source of the truth which they had previously ignored or denied.

This was not Khomiakov's position. He was never outside the Church; it was for him his true and only home. That is why he could speak in its name with authority and a freedom which sometimes even shocked his newly converted friends. He was so deeply rooted in the life of the Church, so certain of the truth of its teaching, that he was not afraid to be outspoken in his criticism of the failures and shortcomings of its leaders and members. He was convinced that any attempt to conceal the defects of Church life was a proof of disbelief in its divine power. His fearless criticism caused him much trouble, and he gained the reputation of a dangerous freethinker, even of an atheist, among the conservatives of the Court. His writings seemed so provocative and revolutionary to his contemporaries just because he was the mouthpiece of the living Church, and never used the dead language of those theologians who only repeat the utterances of other Christians.

Khomiakov's name is associated with the Russian school of thought known as the Slavophil movement. His contributions to it were decisive, and he in his turn was profoundly influenced by it. It is therefore impossible to form any picture of his teaching and personality without some acquaintance with the origin and character of that movement.

The Slavophils and their opponents, the Westernisers, appeared on the scene of Russian history late in the first half of the nineteenth century. It was a time of political reaction, when Nicholas I (1825–55) was trying to keep order in Russia by means of military parades and governmental regulations produced by an army of State officials. Every form of private initiative was discouraged, every expression of independent thought was suppressed, every attempt at criticism, from whatever quarter it came, was punished.

This compulsory silence was imposed upon the country just at the time when Russia had more men who were worth listening to and had the desire and ability to speak and write than at any other period of her history. It was the time of Russia's greatest poet, Alexander Pushkin (1799–1837); in those years Nikolai Gogol (1809–52) and Mikhail Lermontov (1814–44) were still alive. The same period witnessed the appearance of a group of young Russians who by their education, moral integrity and intellectual gifts deserved to take a leading part in the life of their nation. They were all animated by the desire to serve their people, and in other countries their social position and ability would have opened to them the gateway to a successful career. But not in the Russia of Nicholas I. The Emperor had no place for such men in his service. He mistrusted and disliked their independence of mind, and the road to governmental and academic appointments was blocked to them. They were gentlemen, all had some money and much leisure, and so, debarred from the work they wanted to do, they gave themselves to endless conversations—the only activity left open to their able and well-trained minds. The old capital, Moscow, was the home of many of these men, and their crowded drawing-rooms became the scene of the most brilliant and animated debates the country had ever heard. They were all strongly influenced by the philosophy of the Germans—especially

Schelling and Hegel—and their main interest was centred in the problem of religion, of culture and of the destiny of Russia and of Europe. One of their group, Iuri Samarin (1819–76), in one of his letters, gives the list of some of the subjects discussed in Moscow in those years. He wrote: "We used to argue about the relation between Orthodoxy, Latinism and Protestantism. Is Orthodoxy the undifferentiated and primitive form of Christianity from which the other and higher expressions of religion have arisen through the process of evolution; or is Orthodoxy the unchangeable fullness of religious truth, whilst Christianity in the West has been drawn to opposite poles under the influence of Latin and Germanic traditions? What is the difference between the Russian and the European cultures? Does their divergence depend on the degree of their present development, or is it rooted in the character of their very principles? Must the Russian culture be increasingly swamped, not by the external achievements only of the West, but also by its fundamental outlook; or is it its task to penetrate deeper into the essence of its own Orthodoxy, and there to discover the foundations for the building up of a new, universal culture?"

Such were the questions debated in Moscow towards the middle of the last century. Few people outside the circles of the young Russian enthusiasts could then understand the importance of the points under discussion, but it is easier to see their real significance to-day. The turning point in the life of thinking Moscow occurred in 1836, when Pietr Iakovlevich Chaadaev (1793–1856) published in one of the Moscow magazines his "Philosophical Letters." This event helped to disentangle the opposing tendencies of Russian religious and philosophical thought, and Slavophils and Westernisers began to be aware of their affinities and repulsions.

Chaadaev was one of the best-known personalities of Moscow society, well-bred, intelligent and widely read; he had been·described as the only good European that Russia had produced in his generation. He was too critical and too independent for a government post, and therefore lived in retirement in Moscow, where he exercised great influence upon the best minds of the younger generation. He was bold enough to express in public his deep concern about the future of Russia, at a time when enforced silence reigned everywhere and official optimism was the only mood permitted to the Russian people. His article had immediate and drastic effect. The magazine which printed it was suspended, the censor who had allowed its publication was dismissed, and the Emperor, angered by the impertinence of the author, could find no better way of punishing the culprit than to have him declared insane. Chaadaev was forbidden to write again, and for several years had to endure the compulsory visits of a police doctor. But even such measures failed to check his influence; his voice resounded like a sudden alarm breaking the tedium of a long, dark night.

Chaadaev expressed in clear and unmistakable accents general feelings already widely diffused among the Russian admirers and imitators of Europe. He had dared to say in public things which were taken for granted, but never stated in terms, and had forced the Russian upper classes to face all that was implied in the habitual attitude to their own country.

The most striking side of his article, however, was not so much what he wrote as the tone in which he addressed his readers. He broke away from the usual complacency of the Russian Westernised classes and their naïve satisfaction with their European ways and manners; Chaadaev was the first to realise the humiliation of the voluntary surrender of Russia to the West, and he felt both pain and grief at the apparent bankruptcy of his native culture, which had been at once the pretext and the consequence of that surrender. He wrote: "We have given nothing to the world, and learned nothing from it. A thousand years of Russian history is a blank page, on which nothing worth remembering has been recorded." For him the movement of history had been confined to the West, where the human mind had come to maturity under the leadership of the Roman Church. Russia had no culture, for she had remained outside that process.

Chaadaev's charges stirred all that was intellectually vital in Russia. Everybody was discussing his article, and its effects were particularly profound upon those young Moscow intellectuals who were already engrossed in the discussion of this very problem. Alexander Herzen wrote: "It was an agonised cry of pain and shame wrung from the Russia of Peter the Great's reforms. . . . From the first page, I was struck by his grave and sad tone, every word breathed suffering long endured. It was an indictment of all Russia. Twice I had to stop to regain my breath and calm my thoughts and feelings." Such was the response to Chaadaev's words, and at once a sharp cleavage showed itself between two groups among the readers.

One group, the Westernisers, took Chaadaev's side. They agreed with him that the Western civilisation *was* civilisation *tout court*, and that Russia had no other future short of her absorption in the life of Europe. Their religious, political and social ideals were all borrowed from Western sources and they believed that Russia could be progressive and prosperous only when she became without qualification European. Their opponents were the Slavophils. They too loved and admired Europe, but they were convinced that Russian culture had secured many values almost undreamed of by the West. They wanted to see their country develop its own tradition, and they believed that it had much to teach other nations. The Church they held to be the source of all that was positive and creative in Russian life, and Orthodoxy they considered to be superior to Western forms of Christianity.

At first both parties shared to some extent a similar outlook, being under the common influence of German idealism, but gradually the gap between them widened till a state of bitter and open warfare was declared. Ties of personal friendship had once united the Westernisers like Alexander Hertzen (1812–70) and Nikolai Ogarev (1813–77), with Slavophils like Ivan Kireevski (1806–56), Pietr Kireevski (1808–56), Constantin Aksakov (1818–60), Ivan Aksakov (1823–86), Nikolai Iazykov (1803–46), Alexander Koshelev (1806–83) and Iuri Samarin (1819–76). These were now broken. The Westernisers gradually renounced their philosophical idealism, and became revolutionaries and atheists. The Slavophils changed less, till in the latter half of the nineteenth century the movement fell into the hands of men like Mikhail Katkov (1820–87), N. Strakhov (1828–96) and N. Danilevski (1822–85), who began to preach an aggressive nationalism under the name of Slavophilism. Their outlook had little in common with the teaching of the founders of the movement, but few of these lived long enough to see the new use of the name so dear to them.

Originally the Slavophils were a small close-knit group of personal friends, sharing the same interests and outlook. They were treated as eccentrics by their own class, disliked and suspected by the Court, watched by the police, ostracised by the liberal and revolutionary circles. But undismayed by this general opposition, misunderstood and calumniated, they continued to preach their doctrine, proclaiming their belief in the vigour and originality of Russian culture, and putting their trust in the truth of Christian teaching as revealed by the Orthodox Church. Alexei Khomiakov was the centre of the whole movement. He was the greatest man among them, both as a person and as a thinker, and all recognised him as their leader; whilst others might be experts in some particular branch of philosophy, history or economics, his interest embraced every question, practical, historical, philological or theological, which concerned the movement.

Khomiakov was a born speaker and a brilliant dialectician. If the Russia of his time had had free political institutions, his voice would have resounded in the councils of Church and State, and his fame spread far and wide. But Khomiakov lived at a time when his words were silenced, his movements censured and his actions forbidden. He could therefore share his creative thought only with the small circle of his intimate friends.

These, however, were so impressed with his ideas that they urged him to put them into writing. Khomiakov was not a writer, but a speaker; however, under this friendly pressure, he did put on paper some of his convictions and observations. His works were collected by his followers and published in eight volumes in 1900. They form only a fragment of the theological and philosophical intuitions which he poured out with such eloquence in the drawing-rooms of his beloved Moscow. Nevertheless, his writings contain enough material for the study of his philosophy, and they provide an estimate of his integrity and originality. During his lifetime only a few of his articles passed the censor; several of his books and pamphlets had to be published abroad; yet in these fugitive contro-versial writings Khomiakov was the first to express in terms familiar to modern European thought fundamental convictions of the Russian Orthodox mind. This retired Guardsman, brought up by a French abbé, bred up to mathematics in Moscow and to painting in Paris, became the chief exponent of the Slavophil philosophy of life and at the same time the first original theologian and authentic spokesman of the Russian Church.[1]

[1] It may at first appear strange that Khomiakov, a layman who had never had any regular theological education, should yet be the first original theologian of the Russian Church. This is not, however, entirely unaccountable, in the light of its peculiar history. The Russians had neither theological schools nor theology, as it is understood in the West, until the eighteenth century. Theo-logical seminaries were introduced into Russia, together with other innovations, by Peter the Great. The reforming Tsar was in such a hurry to bring into being a new European Russia that he had no time to take into account how far the new institutions were suited to Russian conditions. The Russian theological schools were copied from Western models; yet, though the books and methods of instruction were all Western, they were neither Roman nor Reformed. Latin doctrines were taught, only to be refuted by arguments borrowed from the Protestants, whilst Protestantism was criticised from the standpoint of the Roman theologians. Everything in these schools was Western; even the language of instruction was Latin. They were entirely foreign to Russian soil and could neither grow nor produce genuine fruit. By the middle of the nineteenth century

His analysis of the situation was acute, his warning against coming dangers timely. Yet he was ignored by his contemporaries, forgotten by the next generation and rediscovered only in the twentieth century. His attitude to Russia, to Europe and to the task of the Church was truly prophetic, for he foresaw the events of our own time, and suggested a course of action which there may yet be time to adopt.

The basic intuition of Khomiakov's thought, the driving power behind his religious, political and economic ideas, was his conception of man as an "acting reason," or a "reasoning will" (I, 283).[1] By using this definition of man, Khomiakov expressed his conviction that knowledge and action were inseparable, that man could understand reality only in so far as he was determined to act, and only those actions were effective which were the fruit of his reasoning. Khomiakov stood in irreconcilable opposition to the predominant tendency of his time to split man's faculties up into different departments and treat his reason, will and emotions as independent of each other.

He was equally opposed to the idea that man could be segregated from the cosmos whose organic part he was. He believed that only by being attuned to the laws of the universe could a human being grow into a matured person, and make full use of his creative power. The cosmos was not to Khomiakov an outcome of the play of

they had a hundred years of tradition behind them. Many of the professors and students were gifted and devout, but they were intellectually alienated from their own Church, without ever becoming really at home in the Western world. Roman Catholic and Protestant theology was growing normally, but the Russian theological schools had no life of their own, and were hopelessly out of touch with the newer currents both of Western and Russian thought. In the nineteenth century they were still repeating the arguments of the eighteenth. The Russian clergy brought up in these schools were imbued with Western ideals already a hundred years out of date.

Their theology, therefore, was alien to the contemporary world, their thought and language unfamiliar to the simple believers of their own Church, and their message, accordingly, lacked at once relevance and authority. Khomiakov had both, for he knew the idiom of his contemporaries and social equals, and drew his intellectual nourishment from the same sources as the mass of the Orthodox faithful. Such were the circumstances that made him the first authentic theologian of Russian Orthodoxy.

[1] All further quotations are made from the edition of 1900 and refer to the volume and page of that edition.

blind forces; it was the creation of a "willing reason," infinitely superior to man, but not fundamentally alien to him, since human beings were shaped according to the Divine prototype and reflected the life of the Creator.

"The world is a creation, it is a Divine thought, it represents a complete and perfect harmony of beauty and joy. A spirit that violates the law of Divine truth and righteousness puts himself in a state of hostility towards this Divine thought, towards the harmony of cosmic life, and is therefore bound to suffer" (VIII, 358). Man's intellectual power depends, therefore, on his unconstrained submission to the laws which govern the creation, and among these the first and highest is the principle of love. As reason is bound to will, so knowledge depends on love. Love cannot be but between two; and so thought is a common work. "Accord with love alone can strengthen and enlarge our mental vision. We must submit to the law of love, and attune to it the persistent disharmony of our intellectual powers."

"Love is not a tendency towards unification; it requires, it seeks, it creates responses and contacts. Love itself grows and is strengthened and perfected through these responses and communications."

"The communion of love is indispensable for the understanding of truth; all true knowledge is based on love, and is unobtainable without it."

"The highest knowledge of truth is beyond the reach of an isolated mind; it is open only to a society of minds bound together by love. Truth looks as though it were the achievement of the few, but in reality it is the creation and possession of all" (I, 283).

The main practical consequence of such a conception of man was Khomiakov's recognition of the organic unity of all human beings. An isolated and self-sufficient individual was a sick being, who stood in opposition to the laws of creation. His intellect, his emotions, his will-power, were all distorted and misdirected. However gifted and strong was such a man by nature, he was fundamentally powerless, for he was cut off from the main stream of life.

"The loneliness of a man is the cause of his impotence; whosoever separates himself from people creates a desert around him" (I, 90).

"Only in living communion with others can a man break out of the deadly loneliness of egotistic existence and gain the standing of a living organ in the great organism" (I, 101).

"A self-centred individual is powerless; he is a victim of irreconcilable inner discord" (I, 161).

The moral and intellectual growth of a man was impossible without his willing co-operation with others.

The same rule applied to all works of science and art. Khomiakov drew a distinction between living and decaying, science or art: the first were the creation of healthy minds, the second of the sectarian minds of self-centred people. Artists and scientists were not independent agents; their task was to serve and edify the community, and from that source they had to draw their inspiration.

"Art is free only when the artist gives up his freedom" (III, 372). "A man who wants to develop his latent creative forces must first sacrifice the selfish side of his personality and thus penetrate into the mystery of common life. He must be united with it by the ties of a living organic fellowship" (I, 92).

"A single intellect segregated from living contact with others is barren; only from communion with life can it increase in power and creativeness" (I, 85).

This emphasis on unity was in no way a denial of personality or moral responsibility. On the contrary, the closer the co-operation between the individual and the community, the richer and the fuller would the life of a man become.

"However great our contribution to the common stock, we get back a hundred times more than we give" (I, 101).

Khomiakov was a shrewd observer of life: its every manifestation in art, science, economics or politics fascinated him, attracted his attention, and stimulated him to action. He had many gifts and could express his personality with equal facility through writing a poem, painting a picture, or improving a steam engine. He knew himself and other people well, and his historical and philosophical essays reveal a remarkable grasp of psychology and a vast knowledge of the human background. He was free from sentimentality, and never suffered from any tendency to idealise mankind. He knew well how strong and deeply-rooted was selfishness in every human being, and never dreamed that man alone and unaided could ever transcend his egocentric existence and enter into willing co-operation with others.

Khomiakov's hope of the ultimate victory of love over hate and fear was based, not on any confidence in man's capacity for self-improvement, but on faith that the Creator of the Universe has provided man with the necessary means of combating selfishness and sin.

The most powerful of such means was to him the fellowship of the Christian Church. Khomiakov's statement on the nature and purpose of the Church was the most valuable part of his work. He touched on this theme in many of his writings, but the fullest treatment of it was given in his famous essay, *The Church is One*. He ascribed great importance to it, and it was one of the sorrows of his life that he was not able to see it published. It was printed first in Berlin in 1867, and was allowed to appear in Russia only in 1879. His doctrine on the Church was further elaborated in several controversial articles on the Western Churches. These were all published abroad and later collected in a single volume, *L'Eglise Latine et le Protestantisme*, Lausanne, 1872.

Khomiakov's ecclesiology was organically connected with his anthropology. His view of the Church was of a piece with his view of the nature of man. Many of his definitions of the Church sounded novel and provocative: they differed so radically from the accepted point of view that the first impression his works produced was that of a challenging innovation, a drastic departure from the traditional outlook.

Nothing could be further from the truth. Khomiakov did not invent a theory of his own. He expressed in his writings the traditional teaching of Eastern Orthodoxy. The revolution he caused was due to his breaking away from the decadent Western scholasticism which had for so long dominated theological schools of Russia and Greece, and made the works of even gifted Orthodox writers dull and lifeless. Khomiakov brushed aside all that was alien to Eastern thought. In his books Orthodox theology appeared at last in its proper form. The fault was in his readers if they failed to recognise the patristic thought in the secular idiom of the nineteenth century. The Church, for Khomiakov, was neither a doctrine, nor a system of ecclesiastical government, nor an institution. She was the first-fruit of the new order to come in which men would be restored to harmony with the Creator, and recover their fellowship with one another.

The Church anticipates the fuller and richer life which God had meant for men, but which men unredeemed could not attain. Only in the Church can man find himself, and establish right relations with the rest of creation, for within her fold his heart, mind and will are regenerated and purified and his being made whole by the action of the Holy Spirit.

The Church is a free gift from above, the most powerful manifestation of the Holy Ghost in the life of the creation, but men can appropriate this gift only if they willingly submit themselves to the Divine rule.

The Church being the organism of love, requires of its members complete freedom and the full use of their reason. Every form of constraint, oppression and discord is contrary to its nature.

The Church is a perfect unity, but its oneness is different from that of any other type of social organisation known to men. To describe this difference, Khomiakov laid special stress on the word *sobornost*, which stands for "catholic" in the Slavonic text of the Nicene Creed. Khomiakov was a keen philologist. The word *sobórnost*, derived from the root *sobirat*, "to bring together," suggested much to him; it meant that the Church was catholic, not so much because it was spread all over the world as because it brought into one all men, and all in men. In its fellowship each may find the fullest expression of his personality, for it is unity in freedom, as opposed to uniformity and compulsion (II, 311-14).

Only such a unity can be of any benefit to men. "The unity of the Church," wrote Khomiakov in his essay, *The Church is One*, "follows of necessity from the unity of God; for the Church is not a multitude of people in their separated individualities, but the oneness of Divine grace indwelling in reasonable creatures who freely submit themselves thereto" (II, 3).

The free consent of reasonable and fully responsible persons is the human response to the call of the Holy Spirit, but the Church itself is prior to that response. It is a part of a new and higher order, and lives and moves by the grace of God. "Even on earth the Church lives not an earthly human, but a Divine and blessed life. She triumphantly calls 'holy' not only each of her members, but herself in her entirety. Her visible manifestations are the Sacraments, her inner life consists in the gifts of the Holy Spirit, in faith, hope and charity" (II, 17).

"She lives not under the law of slavery, but that of freedom; she recognises no authority but her own, no judgment but the judgment of faith (for reason cannot apprehend her), and she expresses her charity, her faith and hope in prayers and rites inspired by the Spirit of truth and by the grace of Christ" (II, 17).

"We know that if one of us falls, he falls alone, but no one can be saved alone. Those who are saved are saved within the Church as her members in unity with all the rest. If anyone has faith, he shares a common faith; if he loves, he shares love; if he prays, he shares the prayer of all the rest" (II, 21).

"The Church prays for all, and together we all pray for all. We pray in the spirit of love, and not that of calculation, in the spirit of freedom of sons, and not that of an hireling asking for pay. Everyone

E

who asks, 'What can it profit me to pray?' confesses himself a
slave, for the true prayer is true love" (II, 23). Such a view of the
Church stood in sharp contrast with current doctrines on the
Church professed among Western Christians. Khomiakov was
well aware of this, and emphasised the difference by comparing
what he described as the true and the defective conceptions of the
Church. He wrote: "'The Church is authority,' said the famous
French historian Guizot, a poor Roman Catholic! The Church is
not authority, as God is not authority, as Christ is not authority,
for authority is external to its subjects. The Church is truth and
life. She is the inner life of a Christian, more intimate than the
blood in his veins" (II, 54).

The Roman Catholic distinction between clergy, who alone
have the right to teach, and laity, whose duty is to obey, he emphatically repudiated. According to him, every Christian was
a teacher of truth. "A martyr dying for his faith, a judge rightly
dispensing justice (not for the sake of men, but for the sake of
God), a ploughman in his humble work constantly raising his
mind to his Creator, all alike live and die as teachers of their
brethren" (II, 61).

"The Church knows brotherhood, but not subjection" (II, 69).
Such denials of the need of authority might well seem to Western
ears to undermine the unity of the Church, and endanger the
purity of her doctrine. Khomiakov's answer to these doubts was
that "The strength of the Church lies in the mutual love of her
members; her weapon against heresies is the communion of prayer.
God's help will never be wanting to love and prayer, for both are
inspired by Him" (II, 59). He knew that on that point he touched
one of the most delicate and controversial problems of ecclesiology,
and in support of his thesis he quoted the Encyclical of 1848 signed
by the Eastern Patriarchs and issued in reply to Pius IX. This
document confirmed the ideas so dear to Khomiakov, "That
infallibility resides solely in the Œcumenical fellowship of the
Church, united together by mutual love, and that the guardianship
of dogmas and of the purity of rites is entrusted, not to the hierarchy
alone, but to all members of the Church, who are the Body of
Christ" (II, 60). Accordingly, to Khomiakov, the Church had no
need of any external guarantee of its orthodoxy and unity; only
the mutual love among its members could render them immune
to heresy or discord.

"The true Church has no place for the 'teaching Church'"
(II, 61). Her orthodoxy depended on no other power than the

willing response of the Christians to the guidance of the Holy Spirit.

Khomiakov did not describe the Church from the point of view of an outsider; he was not a mere learned observer of its life. He himself was a living member of the Church, and therefore its true spokesman. Samarin, in his preface to Khomiakov's theological works, rightly described his friend and teacher as "a Doctor of the Church" (II, xxxvi), and his justification was that Khomiakov "lived in the Church" (II, x), and the Church lived in him.

In the light of such an understanding of human nature and of the task which men had to achieve with the help of the Church, it was obvious that Khomiakov could find little sympathy for the course taken by European civilisation. More than that, he was convinced that the West was rapidly heading towards collapse and disintegration.

For the majority of his contemporaries Khomiakov looked almost like a crank. At a time when political and economic progress seemed to be secure, when European nations were rendering tributary the whole world, and everyone prophesied the advent of a new era of unprecedented prosperity, happiness and freedom, Khomiakov had the audacity to preach the approaching downfall of European civilisation, and was bold enough to predict the coming enslavement of proud Western man.

The nineteenth century in Europe was dominated by the ever-increasing assertion of individualism. The popular slogans of all progressive movements claimed the emancipation of man from the shackles of tradition; they advocated freedom of thought, feeling and action. Hope for a better future was pinned on the denial of the right of the community to control the life of individuals.

Khomiakov stood in direct opposition to this current of thought. The triumph of individualism meant for him, not an advance, but disintegration; it carried with it the collapse of man's creative power, and the loss of his true freedom. "Modern society in its decay releases every individual to the freedom of his own impotence" (III, 356). Such was Khomiakov's dark view of European progress. Yet he was not reactionary. Neither did he romanticise the past, as other Slavophils were inclined to do. His will was turned to the future, and a better and more glorious future than anything ever experienced by mankind.

He believed in the possibility of improvement, and he ardently defended freedom. But he was convinced that the road chosen by Europe was bound to lead to disaster, and only on this ground was he opposed to the progressive movements of his time.

Khomiakov's criticism was unsparing, his attacks vigorous, but they were the outcome of his profound attachment to culture, and his deep-rooted trust in man. "Our principles," he wrote in a letter to Samarin, "are as far removed from conservatism with its ridiculous one-sidedness as from the revolutionary movement with its immoral and passionate self-reliance. We stand for intelligent progress against wandering at random" (VIII, 251).

Khomiakov's criticism of European civilisation was not concerned with any of its particular political and social manifestations; it went to the very root of its origins. He was convinced that the cause of its one-sided development lay in the defective interpretation of Christianity inherited by the West from Rome.

The Roman Catholic system of doctrine and practice has been the object of many bitter assaults from the most diverse quarters. Atheists and deists, protestants and rationalists, anti-sacramentalists and pietists have fought against Rome, and ridiculed the Papacy; but Khomiakov's opposition to that institution was different. It arose from the depth of his spiritual and sacramental experience in the Orthodox Church. His protest was made, not in the name of an individual whose reason or will were unable to accept the Roman claims, but as the outcome of belief in the corporate nature of mankind, and in the special task assigned by God to Christians. Christianity was for Khomiakov "the supreme revelation of freedom and creativeness in men" (VI, 448). Men's hope of overcoming their self-centredness, and of achieving harmony with their Creator, depended solely on the Christian religion. In order to reach perfect unity among themselves, men had to be assisted by the Church in the full exercise of its creative power. This meant that the Church had to be the pattern of harmony, unity and freedom.

According to him, the Roman Church had failed to preserve this high standard. It had become a victim of a heresy which had distorted its life, and in consequence had misdirected the whole evolution of European civilisation.

The Roman heresy was not directed against God or Christ; it was a heresy against Christian fellowship; it was a social heresy, and therefore it affected mainly the corporate life of Western society, encouraging the growth of pride, aggressive individualism and exaggerated rationalism. Khomiakov saw the first signs of this social disease already in the early stages of Latin Christianity. The idea of fellowship based on common faith, cemented by love and realised in complete freedom was hard to accept for the men brought up in the traditions of Imperial Rome. "The deification of political society is the essence of Roman culture. Western man was so impressed with it that he could not conceive even the Church save under the form of a State. Her unity had to be compulsive, and hence was born the Inquisition, with its control of conscience, and with its executions for misbelief. The Bishop of Rome was obliged to claim civil power, and eventually he secured it. He acquired the right of juridical control over the part of the Church which became known under the name 'Roman.' Political unity requires the unity of language, and the Latin tongue obtained that status" (I, 207).

"The Church, from being a living community governed by the free consent of her members, became a State; lay people became obedient subjects, and the hierarchy their governors" (VII, 448).

"The life of the Church was to such an extent centred in the clergy that the very symbol of life, the Blood, was refused to laity in the Sacrament of the Eucharist" (VII, 450).

The Roman Church ceased, for its members, to be the school of communal life in unity and freedom. It became exacting and disciplinarian, the sponsor of intolerance and compulsion. The Church blessed the Crusaders, who by the power of the sword sought to restore the rule of the Christian in the Holy Land. It approved the military monastic orders, which offered the choice of baptism or death to the defeated. It welcomed the work of the Jesuits, who fostered rivalries and disintegration among the non-papal Christians (I, 207).

All these distorted manifestations of Christian zeal were the unfortunate results of the confusion between free Christian fellowship and compulsive political unity. Yet this fatal development was not inevitable. The Western Christians were the victims of their own mistake. They themselves deliberately embarked on this road of disregard for true brotherhood. The evil choice was made by them at the time of their separation from communion with the Christian East.

The long rivalry between Rome and Constantinople, which ended in the open breach of 1054, has been the subject of many studies and of a vast controversial literature. Khomiakov, in his interpretation of its causes, did not follow the beaten track. His view of the schism was characteristically fresh and stimulating. Instead of weighing the theological arguments for the single or double procession of the Holy Spirit, which has been the accepted pretext of the schism, he treated it as a glaring example of un-brotherly conduct by one part of the Church towards another. Khomiakov's contention was that the Western Christians had let themselves be led away by pride and lust for power. They had introduced the *Filioque* clause into the Nicene Creed without the consent of their Eastern brothers and, when the Orthodox pro-tested, had insisted on their right to do so. The text of the so-called Nicene Creed did not cover all the doctrines of the Church, and even those it did could be stated with further detail and precision so that its alteration was theoretically conceivable. The text had, however, been accepted by the Orthodox and Latin Christians as their common profession of faith, and they had solemnly pledged themselves neither to alter nor add to it without mutual consent. It was a free moral agreement and a token of brotherly trust and equality between members of the Church. When, therefore, the West altered the Creed by its own decision in the eighth century, the Roman world declared "that in its eyes the whole East was no more than a body of helots in matters of faith and teaching. This was the end of the life in the Church for half her members" (II, 50).

Khomiakov accused the West of surrendering Christian fellow-ship to self-asserting pride. The Catholics had allowed local and individual opinion to triumph over the common mind of Christians. It was the beginning of fratricide between members of the Church, and the West was the first to suffer from its consequences, for the initiative had come from it. Khomiakov never missed an oppor-tunity of emphasising the importance of the schism for the history of Christendom. He showed no mercy to the Papacy, laying on it the whole blame, and exonerating the East from the spirit of schism. From this point of view, his presentation of the conflict was biassed. But his main thesis that the Roman tendency to centralisation and the abuses resulting from it were consequences of the isolation of the West from the East was historically sound. He was the first theologian who brought out the moral principle at work in an event which had hitherto been explained in terms either of doctrinal controversy or of personal quarrels between ambitious prelates.

Equally original was Khomiakov's description of the Protestant reaction to Rome. He entirely disagreed with the common point of view which contrasted the two types of Western Christianity, and described Catholicism as social and Protestantism as individualistic forms of religion. On the contrary, Khomiakov treated papalism as the first manifestation of individualism in the life of the Church. The Popes had set themselves above the community; they had usurped the power which belonged originally to the entire fellowship; they had replaced the system of consultation and common decision by their own personal rule.

The Protestants, according to Khomiakov, had carried the process a stage further by declaring that not only the Popes, but every Christian, stood above the community and its tradition and was a law to himself. The rationalism of the Reformed Christians, the inevitable outcome of individualism, was the completion of Roman rationalism. It differed from the latter only by its more radical character, but it had sprung from the same cause (VIII, 213).

The Christians of the West were caught in a vicious circle. The reaction at the time of the Reformation against the excessive claims of the Popes went amiss, for it sprang from the wrong spirit. Protestantism was nothing more than papal individualism brought to its logical conclusion. Rome had imposed upon the Christian West unity without freedom; the Protestants achieved freedom, but at the expense of unity. Yet neither unity without freedom nor freedom without unity was of any use (II, 212). They both meant the isolation of man, and his exclusion from the redeeming influence of true Christian fellowship. The West had rejected the fundamental teaching of love, on which the whole life of the Church was based.

This error exposed the very principle of Christian solidarity to the attacks of disbelief exactly in the same way as the God-man, who was the Incarnate Love, was betrayed by men. "In our days as in the past, the High Priest (Rome) tries to subjugate Christ to the outward law, and the sceptic, the pupil of Greece (Protestantism) enquires, 'What is truth?' and is unable to comprehend it; and both, the High Priest and the sceptic Pilate, deliver Him into the hands of unbelief which prepares for Him torture and the Cross" (II, 245).

It was a severe and not a discriminating judgment on Western Christianity. Khomiakov saw a great and inspiring vision of the Church as "the revelation of the Holy Ghost given to the mutual love of Christians" (II, 222). He described love as "the burning gift from above which alone can secure to man the unconditional knowledge of Truth" (II, 108), and this made him impatient with the shortcomings of the West. His criticism of the actual state of the divided Churches was trenchant and often true, but his logic carried him too far. Such was the case when he saw in Rome only oppression, in Protestantism only rationalism (II, 214), and described the Anglican Church, which he loved best among the Western Churches, as "a sand dune in the midst of a sea, rapidly disappearing under the pressure of the conflicting waves of Romanism and Dissent" (II, 213).

The sorrow he felt at the failures of Europe made him blind to the power of grace, faith and love among the members of the Western Churches. And his zeal for Christian truth as taught him by his own Church made him reluctant to recognise that Eastern Orthodoxy suffered also from the same defects which he so acutely felt in other Churches. His fundamental mistake consisted of using two standards. He described the Roman Catholics and the Protestants in their actual historical position with all their limitations, whilst he approached the Orthodox Church from the point of view of her ideals and aspirations, paying too little attention to the gap between the ultimate goal and its concrete realisation.

He was fighting a lonely battle; he stood alone in defence of the much-maligned and much-misunderstood Orthodox Church, and therefore he overstressed the fact that Eastern Christians faithfully preserved the true vision of the Church in spite of all their historical calamities and shortcomings.

Only a few of his friends, like Alexander Koshelev, for instance, objected to Khomiakov's biassed attitude towards the Western Churches; the majority of the Slavophils were carried away by their leader's eloquence and strength of conviction, with the result that the vitality of the movement in the next generation was undermined by intolerance and narrow nationalism. But all these limitations of Khomiakov's outlook must not obscure the all-important fact that he was able to formulate the doctrine of the Church more adequately than was customary in the theological manuals and schools of his generation. Khomiakov's works were a great step forward towards the establishment of mutual understanding among Christians; for his conception of the Church required the unity of her members. It was one of the greatest paradoxes of Khomiakov's life that the man who attacked most bitterly the Western Christians was at the same time the first Eastern theologian who felt a genuine concern for the Churches of the West and realised the grave sin of divisions.

Surrounded by the indifference, suspicion and prejudices of his time, Khomiakov tried to arouse the members of the Russian Church from their apathy towards reunion. He wanted to make them realise their responsibility for the fate of other Christians, but his efforts ended in failure. The East was not yet ripe for action. His correspondence with William Palmer (*d.* 1879), an Anglican deacon and theologian, a Fellow of Magdalen College, Oxford, formed the most important page in the history of Anglican-Orthodox relations in the first part of the nineteenth century.[1]

Khomiakov felt a warm affection for his friend and was deeply hurt when both Russian and Greek hierarchs displayed complete indifference to Palmer's case and made no effort to meet his desire to become an Orthodox. Palmer eventually joined the Roman Catholic Church, but remained till his death absorbed in studies of Russian history.[2]

Khomiakov loved Europe. He felt pain at seeing her moving along the road to disaster, and with his whole heart he believed that Russia would be able to escape the tragic fate of the West, and eventually to help other nations to recover the fullness of Christianity.

"We Russians do not belong to this doomed world, and we can say so while yet paying due respect to all that is great in European achievements in art, science and history" (III, 211).

His faith in the great destiny of the Orthodox Slavs was based on two features of their history and outlook. As nations, they were not polluted by the lust for conquest; their past was not stained by the violation of the freedom and integrity of their neighbours; and as Christians, they were members of a Church which was purer in her life and teaching than the Western Confessions, and less affected by secularism and institutionalism.

Khomiakov was a diligent student of history. His essays on "Universal History," published in Vols. V, VI and VII of his works, were full of stimulating suggestions, and original intuitions. He read all the available historical literature of his time, and made good use of it. His criticism of contemporary Western historians was that they paid disproportionate attention to outward events, being concerned mostly with States, their wars and politics, while

[1] Their correspondence was published by J. Birkbeck, *Russia and the English Church*, London, 1895.

[2] Palmer published in 1871-6 *The Patriarch and the Tzar*, a study of the origin of the Russian schism of the seventeenth century (in six volumes).

almost ignoring the more significant inner history of the human race. This inner history, according to Khomiakov, consisted of two all-important elements: religious convictions and racial and national characteristics. The two were closely interwoven, and found their concrete expression in the different social structures evolved by the nations. His attention was particularly attracted to the tension between the Germanic and the Slavonic peoples, who, in spite of being lifelong neighbours, had found it impossible to live at peace with one another. Khomiakov believed that the root cause of their never-ceasing conflicts lay in their opposite mentality on social matters. The order which had always inspired the Germanic peoples was that of a military brotherhood aiming at the conquest of others. The Slavs had always formed agricultural communities, and had shown no desire to subdue other nations to their will (VII, 393).

He was convinced that the sin of aggression, that violation of harmony and love in the life of mankind, was bound to leave a deep permanent trace in the life of the nations that yielded to it. "People easily forget the facts of past history, but they retain in their souls stubborn traces of the passion which perturbed their ancestors in remote and forgotten ages. A nation of conquerors preserves for ever feelings of pride and contempt, not only towards all the defeated but towards everything foreign" (V, 105).

"An agricultural people stands nearer to the ideal of universal humanity. They are free from the proud charms of victory. They have not seen their enemies prostrate at their feet, turned into slaves by the force of the sword. They are not accustomed to treat themselves as superior to their brothers—other human beings. They are therefore more responsive to influences from outside" (V, 106).

"An Englishman, for instance, does not know the language of the Celts. A Hungarian or a German never speaks the tongue of the oppressed Slavs inhabiting the same land. For us Slavs such pride is incomprehensible. A Slovak usually speaks fluently both German and Hungarian. A Russian looks upon men of all nations inhabiting the great Northern Empire as his brothers. Russians from Siberia often bring into their conversation the dialects of the Siberian nomads, Iakuts and Buriats. A Cossack from the Caucasus will take a wife from a native village of the Chechentsy, a Russian peasant will marry a Tartar or a Mordvin woman. Russia treats as her greatest glory Pushkin, the grandson of a negro, whilst in freedom-loving America he would be denied even citizenship."

"We shall be, as we always have been, the democrats among

European nations. We are the representatives of humanism in its purest form, we wish every other nation a life in freedom and the full development of its own personality" (V, 107).

"Time will show who will take the lead in the further evolution of mankind, but if there is any strength in the brotherhood of the human race, if love, truth and goodness are not phantoms, then not the Germanic conqueror and aristocrat, but the hard-working Slav will be called forth to fruitful exploit and great service" (V, 108).

The peaceful disposition of the agricultural Slavonic people was not however, by itself, enough to make them the promoters of a better international order. Their claims to leadership rested above all on the superiority of their interpretation of Christianity.

Khomiakov ascribed to religion a far-reaching influence on social life. "Faith penetrates into the whole being of man, all his relations with others are coloured by it. Social order is the external manifestation of the inner attitude of men to one another" (I, 385).

In this connection, he believed that Russia stood well. Though she had inherited Christianity from the Byzantine Empire, she had made a new start in the application of religion to the social life of the nation. "The Greeks had succeeded in producing the best intellectual statement on Christian truth. By their achievement they had enriched the life of mankind for all ages. But the Byzantine Empire had failed to show a pattern of a Christian social order" (I, 283).

"Hellenic thought, free and creative in all other spheres of life, in legal matters followed slavishly the road traced by its teachers, the lawyers of Rome. These legalistic chains caught and stifled the life of the Eastern Empire. Christianity could hardly penetrate the majestic stronghold of the lawyers—there the heathen spirit of Rome still reigned supreme" (I, 217).

"The social and political life of Byzantium was thoroughly imbued with the old Roman tradition, which was approved and supported by law and custom alike" (I, 218).

"Christianity was unable to break the solid web of the evil and anti-Christian habits. It retired into the soul of man, and tried to improve personal life, leaving social order untouched" (I, 213).

The Russian people, childlike and unaffected by the Roman tradition, were called to go further; their approach to Christianity from the very beginning was social. In comparison with the rest of Europe, they were backward politically, but in their belief that all spheres of human life must be open to Christian influence, that

Christ's teaching has the same relevance to the social life of mankind as to personal life, they led the way. Already, the first Russian Chronicle, says, "we are all one family, for all have been baptised in the same Christ." This belief in Russia's special mission, which was the inspiring thought behind all Khomiakov's work, was associated in his mind with the community life of the majority of the Russian people. This was, according to him, the Russian attempt to apply the Christian belief in the brotherhood of man to social and economic conditions.

The Russian rural community, the *obshchina*, governed by its popular parliament, the *Mir*, was for Khomiakov no mere remnant of the primitive past, but contained the seeds of a new and higher social order. Such a community was a good school of moral training. Each member realised his interdependence with others, rich and poor belonged to one body, and their personal conduct, the use of the material means at their disposal, their relation to others and to their own families were controlled by public opinion expressed through the village gathering.

Khomiakov attributed particular importance to the widely accepted Russian custom of treating only unanimous decisions as morally binding, since they expressed no longer personal and class interests, but made it possible for people to hear objective truth, the voice of the Holy Spirit. Men in the community lived under the rule of God; they were therefore able to mature more quickly, and to conquer their egoism and pride more easily. Without this discipline of communal life, people were left helpless victims of their passions. Even the good intentions of the better-off towards the poor were of no avail. Khomiakov found the Western notion of philanthropic assistance given to the needy deficient. For it was not the outcome of the vision of the organic unity of mankind, but, all too often, was tainted by fear of the uprising of the poor. It therefore demoralised and humiliated those who had to live on charity, and made those who were unwillingly induced to help others more suspicious and exclusive (III, 466). Community life, with its close interdependence of all, obviated these dangers.

The agricultural *obshchina* was not the only form of communal life known to the Russian people. They also formed numerous small social units called *arteli*. Such was the name given to brotherhoods of artisans, owning small enterprises in common. *Arteli* united carpenters, masons, weavers and millers who preferred to labour and to live together, sharing expenses and profits according to the ability of each member. Khomiakov fully realised that the industrial development of his country was still primitive, yet he believed that the principle exemplified in the *artel* could be applied to a more developed industrial order, and thus save the working classes from proletarianisation, their sad fate in Western Europe (III, 468).

The foundations of a sound Christian order were the greatest possession of the Russian people; they were its guardians for the rest of the world. "Russian life holds many treasures, not for her own people only, but for many others, if not for all nations" (I, 22).

"From Russia, because of its communal outlook, a purer stream of Christianity may flow" (I, 211).

"After a hard struggle, she has saved this principle for herself; now it is time for her to reveal it for the whole world. This is her true calling and her future" (I, 152).

"The idea of an abstract truth has always been foreign to the Russian people; a truth which does not flow from Christ, a justice which contradicts love have never been known in Russia" (I, 246).

"Russian culture puts greater trust in the voice of conscience than in the wisdom of civil institutions" (III, 335).

"The strength of Russia lies in the sanctity of the family circle, and the œcumenical fellowship of the Orthodox Church, which is above all earthly control, in the village community with its unanimous decisions, with its judgment based on the voice of conscience, and on the truth of the heart. These are the greatest treasures of the Russian people" (I, 137-8).

Khomiakov was a great patriot, and for Moscow in particular he felt a deep personal affection. But he was not a narrow-minded chauvinist; he had no illusions as to the grievous shortcomings of his nation, and some of his poems addressed to his country were so sharp in denunciation of its crimes that they brought him much trouble with the authorities. Khomiakov visualised Russia, not in opposition, but in close relation to the rest of the world. Moscow was so dear to him because he believed that his city would become the home of a new social order for all nations. "The interests of Moscow are those of all mankind," he wrote in one of his letters (VIII, 60). The problem of Russia was for him the greatest world problem of modern times; but he was aware that it would not be given to his generation to see her mission fulfilled. "We must remember," he wrote to Samarin in 1845, "that no one of us will survive till the time of harvest, but that our spiritual and ascetic labours of ploughing, sowing and weeding are not for Russia's sake alone, but for the sake of the whole world. This thought alone can give permanence to our efforts" (VIII, 252). Khomiakov attributed a special importance to the fact that the unity of Russian people was based neither on the submission of the conquered to the conqueror nor on any legal contract whereby the rights and duties of conflicting groups were carefully defined. It was, according to Khomiakov, a blessed fruit of the Christian outlook on life accepted by the bulk of the Russian people. It was the result of their voluntary submission to the unique truth of the Gospel. One of the most impressive manifestations of this spiritual unity was for him the sacred pattern of daily life. This pattern—*Obriad*—Khomiakov called Russia's greatest achievement, "the artistic symbol of the inner unity of the nation" (I, 28).

Khomiakov was an exception among the educated Russians in understanding the importance of this common pattern of daily life. For him it was a guarantee of the organic and free unity of a people kept together neither by the pressure of State control nor even by ties of race or language. but by a philosophy of life accessible to the learned and to the simple, since it was expressed, not in text books, but in customs and rites daily observed by men, women and children alike.

When Khomiakov was writing, it was still not only difficult but dangerous to try to elaborate the picture of the social order which he believed corresponded to the true understanding of Christianity. Only once had he any opportunity of doing so. In 1860 he published in Germany an open letter to the Serbians, entitled *An Epistle from Moscow*. He ascribed great importance to it, and he secured for it the signatures of eleven leading members of the Slavophil movement. It was the brotherly advice of Orthodox Christians in Russia to their brethren in Christ living in Serbia, who were engaged in the rebuilding of their political and social life as an independent nation after five hundred years of subjugation to the Turks. This Epistle contained much of what Khomiakov wanted to see realised in his own country. The main emphasis was laid upon the co-operation and brotherhood of all people, which was, however, impossible without economic equality: "Great is the land in which there is neither poverty among the poor, nor luxury among the rich; where life is simple and without display. Such a land is pleasing to God and honoured among men" (I, 401).

Khomiakov wanted the Serbians to avoid Russia's uncritical imitation of Europe. "Our Russian land is like a ship, on board of which only German words of command are heard" (I, 392).

"Let our sad example be a lesson to you; learn from the Western nations as is necessary, but do not imitate them, do not put your trust in them as we in our blindness did. May God keep you from that calamity" (I, 392).

"No one can sing with another's voice, or walk well with another's gait. In the same way the inner life of a nation disintegrates if the stream of foreign thought is allowed to flow unchecked within it" (I, 392).

"Do not hasten to introduce novelties borrowed from other nations unless their usefulness is beyond doubt" (I, 393).

"Do not identify the cunning of the Austrians with culture, and your own simplicity with barbarism" (I, 393).

"Do not be tempted to call yourselves Europeans. This word does not stand for the higher development of the human spirit; value the name of Christian. Do not put a dog-collar neatly labelled 'Europe' on your intellectual freedom" (I, 398).

Khomiakov was aware that no such prohibitive measures as the refusal to allow people to go abroad or to read foreign books could preserve the originality and vigour of a national culture. This could flourish only as the fruit of sound spiritual and social conditions. He was certain that for the Serbians, as for the Russians, the source of their unity and strength lay in their membership of the Orthodox Church.

The Church could be a regenerating and unifying power, however, only if she was free, and therefore religious liberty was one of the first conditions for the growth of her influence.

"Let everybody be perfectly free in the confession of his faith. Let nobody suffer persecution or oppression in his search for God, or worship of Him" (I, 386).

This grant of religious freedom did not mean indifference to religion. Religion was the most important social factor. "Therefore those who do not share the Christian outlook of the nation ought not to be lawgivers, rulers and judges of the nation, for their conscience is different from that of the Christians" (I, 386).

Khomiakov was a realist; he knew that social unity and cooperation were the most vital part of human existence, and he knew also that it could be free and creative only if it was the outcome of the same outlook on life. A society which had lost a common religious background could be kept together only by fear and compulsion. Only a Christian nation could be tolerant, for it had no need to maintain unity by force; the Christians, therefore, had to be watchful and safeguard their spiritual inheritance; and that was why, according to Khomiakov's advice, people who could not share the Christian outlook should be excluded from posts of special moral responsibility in a free Christian country.

Khomiakov ascribed special power to the voice of public opinion as the best weapon for checking undesirable and anti-social tendencies among groups and individuals. "Be severe in the judgment made by public opinion," he advised the Serbians; "without it your customs would be corrupted. But in your legislation be merciful, for in every crime, great or small, the whole community has its share of guilt. Never punish a criminal by death; he cannot resist, and it is a shame to kill a defenceless being. Besides, it is a sin for a Christian to deprive another man of the opportunity for repentance. In the past capital punishment was abolished in the Russian land, and we abhor this penalty. It is still excluded from our civil law. Mercy is the glory of the Orthodox Slavs. It is from the Tartars and the learned Germans that cruelty in punishment penetrated our legislation" (I, 402).

In these words, Khomiakov expressed the traditional revulsion against capital punishment so common to Russian Christians throughout their whole history. He emphasised in his epistle to the Serbians the priority of the social over the political tasks of national reconstruction. The predominance of political interests was to him a disease that Europe had caught from France, and the only Western country which had escaped this danger was England. His frequent references to Great Britain gave him further opportunities for the exposition of his idea of a Christian nation. Khomiakov often sharply criticised England, especially just before the Crimean War (1854-5). He could not understand how a Christian country was prepared to give military assistance to the Turks, the cruel and barbarous oppressors of Christians (III, 184). But he was a man who could feel genuinely hurt by the wrongdoing of those whom he loved and respected. He denounced England because he was so deeply attached to her people. His poem, "The Island," gives his judgment on England. His long and friendly correspondence with William Palmer contained many expressions of Khomiakov's love for this country. But the most interesting analysis of the strength and weakness of England is given in his article, "A Letter on England," which was printed in *The Muscovite* in 1848 (Vol. VII). He was profoundly impressed with his visit to England. He found more in common between Russian and English life than he expected, and the feature which particularly struck him was the existence in England of the same sense of community which he so particularly valued in Russia. He wrote: "I am convinced that, with the exception of Russia, there is no other land in Europe so little known as England" (I, 110).

Khomiakov repudiated the popular notion of the English as a nation of shopkeepers and snobs. He made the interesting observation that English people were not so much politically as socially minded, and that "Tories and Whigs are not political parties in the Continental sense of this word, but two different social outlooks" (I, 124). "In the depth of his heart, every Englishman is a Tory" (I, 124). "An Englishman visits Westminster Abbey neither with the boastful pride of the Frenchman nor with the antiquarian curiosity of a German, but with sincere and ennobling love. There are the tombs of his family—of his great family—and this is felt not only by a lord or a professor, but by an artisan or a cabman" (I, 130).

"The main foundation of English life is religious," and this is true of nowhere else in Europe except Russia. "There is in England a deep and justified mistrust in human reason. This is another common link between Russian and English people. Rationalism is entirely foreign to the English character" (I, 134-5).

Khomiakov was especially impressed with the English Sunday. "I was edified by the empty streets of London on Sunday, and by the complete cessation of all business activities. I was happy to witness the moral will of a nation, the nobility of the human soul. A strange thing, there are people in the world who do not understand and who do not like the Sunday quiet of England. Their lack of appreciation reveals the superficiality of their minds, and the poverty of their souls. Of course, not all the English keep Sunday spiritually. . . . There are hypocrites among individuals, but the nation is not a hypocrite. Weakness and vice belong to single human beings, but the nation recognises above itself a higher moral law, obeys it, and imposes the same obedience upon its members. A German and a Frenchman cannot understand it, but a Russian is familiar with it. Easter day is observed in Russia as strictly as Sunday in England. No songs are sung, no

F

dances are performed throughout the villages of Russia during Lent. Even in the cities all popular amusements are stopped. Of course, a foreigner can say, 'I have no interest in the English Sunday. Why should I have to submit to its control?' This is true but English people believe that they are at home in their own country and they can do there what they like" (I, 109-10).

Khomiakov liked in England the independence of her people, their determination to live their own life, and their freedom from any desire to imitate other nations. But above all, he valued the sound organic structure of its social life. He was certain that Great Britain could withstand better than any other country the coming crisis of Western civilisation.

The crisis Khomiakov predicted has come. The liberal and individualistic civilisation of the West with its trust in the self-sufficiency of man, with its belief in uninterrupted progress, has suffered a severe set-back. The Slavophils' warnings, which sounded so unconvincing to their contemporaries, have turned out to be true. Not all of Khomiakov's predictions have been fulfilled; many of his most cherished expectations still wait their day, and may never be realised, but this does not destroy the importance of his message. A Christian prophet is not a soothsayer; he does not foretell what will happen, but reveals to men the true pattern of their existence as contrasted with their dreams and illusions; he declares to them the will of the Maker of the Universe, as opposed to their own wishes, plans and ambitions. Khomiakov was a genuine prophet because he proclaimed the certainty of the triumph of the Church at a time when it looked little like surviving, let alone outlasting its rivals. Yet his faith was not blind; he saw the same signs of the times as others, only he read them more accurately. Christians in his day were everywhere subjugated to a humiliating State control, and indeed in Russia any independent utterance in religion was forbidden. He had no false illusions about the state of the Church anywhere, and especially in his own country, yet he never lost faith in the Church nor his firm trust in her ultimate victory. At a time when all the progressive and liberal movements were opposed to the Church as a stronghold of reaction, when the majority of Christians were frightened and looked upon the Church as a beleaguered remnant, Khomiakov dared to insist that the Church alone contained the seeds of a new and better order, that she had the keys of the door which social reformers and liberal politicians tried in vain to force.

With unswerving loyalty, he preached that in the Church and not in secularism lay the only hope of freedom for mankind; that social progress was the fruit of Christian living, and those who separated them betrayed their own cause, and were leading Europe into a new and more oppressive slavery.

Khomiakov, however, was not concerned so much with those who left the Church and attacked her from outside as with the re-conversion of Christians themselves. They were the people responsible for the chaos and disintegration of Europe; it was they who lost faith in the guidance of the Holy Spirit, who had become afraid of their own freedom and replaced the rule of self-governing communities by forms of government copied from the pagan State.

Khomiakov was no revolutionary; he did not call upon his followers to attack and destroy the established Church order. His friend Koshelev was right when he wrote that "above all else Khomiakov hated violence" (VIII, 130). If he was opposed to it in politics, even more he considered it out of place in religion. He therefore displayed throughout his life complete obedience to ecclesiastical authority. This was consistent with his whole outlook, for he knew that the old traditional Church, which looked so worn out and decrepit, was the greatest force in the life of mankind, and alone capable of leading it towards a better future. He was certain that nothing could destroy it, that those who fought against it would be defeated, but grave was the sin of those who, instead of using the power given to the Church for social improvement, let it lie idle. With truly prophetic eyes he saw the glory and beauty of the Church in spite of the ugly and degrading dress with which her afflicted body was clothed by her unworthy guardians. Amidst the mockery of sceptics and agnostics and the doubts of hostile and suspicious Christians, Khomiakov continued to preach his doctrine that the Church was called to regenerate the whole life of mankind, that she was an inexhaustible source of strength and inspiration, and that her members ought to be the pioneers of social and economic reconstruction. His teaching has often been denounced as subversive, his insistence on a return to the original freedom of Church was dismissed as impracticable, his social theories were described as naïve and anarchistic.

The leader of the Slavophils was not one of the secular reformers, but a servant of the Living God, and all his daring suggestions for social and economic changes sprang from his belief in the Holy Trinity, the God of love and freedom. To those people who had no such faith, Khomiakov's proposals were bound to appear arbitrary and unconvincing, and his reliance upon men's ability to use properly their freedom full of concealed and open dangers. It is, however, quite a different thing when Khomiakov is assaulted by convinced Christians, for such a criticism raises the fundamental question how far his theology was sound. Was he right or wrong in his description of the relations between God and man, of the task of the Church, and the need for freedom? These questions have not been settled by the corporate mind of the Church and have to be answered by each Christian, but no one who has studied his works could doubt that Khomiakov's solutions were integral, and that they were the fruits of his willing identification of his own personality with the life of Christ's Body.

But even a genuine Christian is but a fallible man. He serves his Master but he is not free from mistakes. Khomiakov was a case in question. He was a sincere Christian, but he was also a man with strong personal likings, with his human hopes, prejudices and limitations, his attacks on Western nations, especially upon the French, for whom he felt little natural sympathy, were biassed. His refusal to recognise that the Christians of the West were members of the same Christian Community to which the Christian East belonged openly contradicted the facts and undermined his own definition of the Church.

Nevertheless, it is quite obvious that in his lifelong controversy against the Westernisers who denied the originality of Russian culture and believed that their country would gradually be turned into a copy of France, Khomiakov was right, and his opponents proved to be surprisingly ignorant of their own national background. They were equally unaware of the nature of the Russian Revolution, for which they laboured with enthusiasm and perseverance. They hoped it would be liberal and individualistic, and open the era of cosmopolitan civilisation in which all national distinction would be lost. Khomiakov expected nothing good from the compulsory overthrow of the State power, but at the same time he had no idea that the Revolution would take the form of Totalitarianism, with its compulsory unity and its atheistic and materialistic collectivism. He belonged still to the well-established world of the nineteenth century, with its security, peace and comfort. He was aware of the approaching crisis, but the face of the new enemy of Christianity which had yet to come he could not clearly see. He still believed that the main foe was the liberal agnostic with his selfishness and scepticism.

Khomiakov was a fierce fighter, a partisan of his cause who was often harsh in his judgments of his opponents, but he was also a generous man, loved not only by his friends, but also by his adversaries. It is remarkable that the best and most recent study of his philosophy has come from a French Roman Catholic, A. Gratieux. He disagrees with much of Khomiakov's criticism of the Latin Christians, but nevertheless is captivated by the breadth of his vision, by his prophetic insight into the future, the dynamism of his Christian faith. Gratieux ends his study with the following words: *"Comment ne pas croire qu'une tel pensée n'a pas été donnée à un grand peuple. Quelles que furent les difficultés, Khomiakov n'aurait jamais perdu confiance. Nous faisons les semailles, disait-il, le moisson sera pour le monde entier."* Gratieux is justified in quoting these words of Khomiakov.

Khomiakov does not belong to Russia only, not even to Eastern Orthodoxy alone. He is a teacher for the whole of Christendom. He was a nationalist, but one who was concerned with the future of all nations; he was a patriot who ardently desired freedom and happiness for every land. He was a revolutionary who was opposed to violence; he was a traditionalist who worshipped freedom; but above all he was a Christian who untiringly fought for the advance of Christ's Kingdom, defending good and opposing evil.

It was not granted to him to witness the victory of the Church; neither could he see the immediate future of his country and the strength of the coming assault of the anti-Christian powers. This knowledge was given to the men of the next generation, and pre-eminently to the most prominent among them—Feodor Mikhailovich Dostoevsky.

Chapter Three

DOSTOEVSKY

WITH Dostoevsky, Russian culture of the nineteenth century reaches its climax. He is one of the greatest novelists the world has known, and one of the most original psychologists of all times. But he is more than a gifted writer; he is also a mystic whose utterances about God and man equal in significance any ever made by a Christian thinker.

He can be compared with a high mountain seen from a distance, which becomes a familiar sight to many people, while remaining a majestic peak never really explored, except by the few audacious climbers who can brave its precipices, its loneliness and its storms, and face the forbidding terrors of its height.

Many books have been written about Dostoevsky, but none has succeeded yet in giving his authentic portrait; in some he appears as a convinced Christian, in others he is described as an atheist. Some emphasise his almost pathological concentration on the morbid side of life; others admire his lucid mind and his ability to disentangle the most perplexing moral problems. He is represented alternatively as the example of the decay of the old Christian world and as the prophet of a new and better order. It would be possible to compose an encyclopædia on psychology, theology and social science out of the material left by Dostoevsky. There is hardly any aspect of man's inner life which was not explored by him, towards the understanding of which he did not make some lasting contributions. His true greatness is better realised with every succeeding generation, but he still awaits an interpreter who will do full justice to the wealth of ideas contained in his writings. This book will study only that section of Dostoevsky's thought which refers to Russia, the West and the future of Christian civilisation. His biography is easily obtainable in English,[1] and therefore only the bare outline of his life need be mentioned here.

---

[1] See monographs by Pfleger, Lavrin and Carr, *Letters*, ed. Mayne, *Letters to his wife*, ed. Hill, and *Diary of Dostoevsky's Wife*. ed. Fülop-Miller.

Feodor Dostoevsky was born in Moscow on October 30th, 1821. His family background stood in sharp contrast to that of Alexei Khomiakov. The Khomiakovs belonged to the old aristocracy, whose roots went deep into their native soil. They were the bearers of the traditional Moscow outlook, genuine spokesmen of Russian culture. The Dostoevskys were a product of the new St. Petersburg Empire. Like many other newcomers who settled down in the old and new capitals of Russia, they belonged to the intelligentsia. Originally the family came from Lithuania. In the seventeenth century one of Feodor's ancestors left his homeland, joined the Orthodox Church and became Russianised. His grandfather, Andrei Dostoevsky, was a priest in Ukraine, his father, Mikhail Dostoevsky, was a military doctor; he married in 1819 Maria Timofeevna Nechaeva, daughter of a Moscow merchant. They had seven children, four sons and three daughters, and Feodor was their second son. Mikhail Dostoevsky was a difficult man. Severe and exacting, he imposed a strict discipline upon his family. He was suspicious and irritable, and his children were often frightened of him.

The mother, Maria Dostoevskaia, who came from a simple home, was a quiet, unassuming woman brought up in the traditional Russian piety. She was a kind mother, but she had no strength to oppose the despotism of her husband. She died prematurely in 1837. After her death, Mikhail Dostoevsky resigned his post in Moscow and retired to his small estate near Tula. There he became even more gloomy and oppressive and, in addition, took to drink. He was murdered by his serfs in 1838.

By that time Feodor had already left his home for St. Petersburg, where he had been sent to study. He was a gifted boy, intelligent and quick, who struck everybody by his vivid imagination. He was passionately fond of reading, and spent all his free time over books. Literature was his only interest, but his father had another plan for his talented son. He wanted to provide him with a secure position, and in 1837 he enrolled him as a student at the College of Military Engineering. Nothing was further from the boy's interests than the career chosen for him by his father. The six years (1838–44) of training were far from being a happy time for him. He kept aloof from the rest of the cadets, and did only the minimum of work. In 1844 he obtained a commission, but he considered his engineering a burden, and devoted his time and energy to reading and writing. Besides such Russian authors as Pushkin and Gogol, Dostoevsky read extensively the works of the Western writers, Dickens, Schiller, Hoffman, and of the French novelists, Balzac, George Sand and Victor Hugo. Literary fame came to Dostoevsky in a sudden and spectacular manner. In 1845 he finished writing his first novel, *Poor Folk*. His friend Grigorovich, also a young writer, took the manuscript to a well-known Russian poet and publisher, Nekrasov. They began to read it together and could not stop till they had finished the story. It was four o'clock in the morning, but they rushed straight to Dostoevsky in order to express their admiration. Dostoevsky was overwhelmed by this visit made at such an unusual hour. He considered this night one of the happiest of his life. This meeting transformed him at once from a junior and not too successful military engineer into a rising star on the Russian literary horizon. His novel was published in 1846, and was greeted as the work of a first-class writer. Dostoevsky was welcomed to the literary circles of the capital. His new career as a novelist seemed to be secure, and he resigned his commission in order to give all his time to what he considered his real work. But he was singularly lacking in practical wisdom, and his precipitate decision to give up a government job proved to be a badly-calculated action.

His second novel, *The Double*, was sharply attacked by the critics. Nekrasov and Belinsky, his former friends, turned against him, and he had to pass through the hard experiences of poverty and frustration. Nevertheless, he continued to write, but none of his further stories met with any success. In the midst of these trials, his work was suddenly interrupted: he was arrested on April 23rd, 1849, accused of political conspiracy, and brought before a court-martial.

The last years of the reign of Nicholas I (1825–55) saw the spread of a particularly oppressive political reaction. The St. Petersburg Government spared no effort in its suppression of the freedom of Russian thought. It believed independent thinking to be the cause of all insubordination and political discontent. Special measures were taken to prevent the Russians from being contaminated by the revolutionary ideas coming from Europe, more particularly from France. Forbidden fruits always appear attractive, and the young men in St. Petersburg and Moscow formed secret circles in order to read and discuss together the latest publications produced in the West. The most popular among them were the theories of French Socialism (Fourier and Saint-Simon). Dostoevsky took part in one of these discussion groups organised by one Petrashevsky. The members of this group were denounced and brought before the court-martial. Twenty of them, including Dostoevsky, were condemned to death. On December 22nd, 1849, they were taken to the place of execution, but at the last moment were reprieved. Dostoevsky was sent instead to Siberia for four years, where he had to endure hard labour. After his release in 1854 he enlisted as a private in one of the Siberian regiments. Gradually his social position was restored. He obtained a commission, married the widow of another officer, and in 1859 was allowed to return to Russia. His life after exile can be divided into three periods. From 1859 till 1865 Dostoevsky was rebuilding his literary reputation and was mostly absorbed in journalism. In 1861, together with his brother Mikhail, he started a periodical called *Vremia*, "The Time." This magazine had considerable success. *The Memoirs of the House of the Dead*, in which Dostoevsky described his experience in Siberia, was particularly well received, and restored his name as a gifted writer. The brothers began to look forward to a secure future. But their hopes were suddenly dashed. The Government took offence at one of the articles, and stopped the publication of the magazine in 1863. After many efforts, the Dostoevskys obtained permission to start another publication, and a new magazine called *The Epoch* appeared in 1864. This time, instead of success, it brought financial ruin. Subscribers were slow to come forward, debts rapidly accumulated, and in the middle of these troubles Mikhail Dostoevsky suddenly collapsed and died, leaving behind a large family and no money. Feodor was absent from St. Petersburg at the time of his brother's death, as he had had to go to Moscow, where his wife was gravely ill. Her death on April 16th, 1864, shortly after the loss of his brother, dealt him another blow. Amidst these misfortunes, Dostoevsky showed strength and perseverance. He tried hard to save *The Epoch*, hoping in this way to provide for the destitute family of his much-loved brother. His efforts came to nothing. The magazine became bankrupt. Considerable debts and the responsibility for numerous relatives were imposed upon a man in ill-health and of no income beyond that from the sale of his novels. Dostoevsky saw only one way to overcome these difficulties: this was to write as much and as quickly as possible and thus find the money which he so desperately needed.

The second period (1865–71) was trying. He had to live abroad in order to escape the danger of imprisonment for his own and his brother's debts. He was constantly imploring his friends to send him money and so to save him from starvation, but he worked hard and during this period produced some of his greatest novels: *Crime and Punishment*, 1866, *The Idiot*, 1868, *The Possessed*, 1870, *Raw Youth*, 1871. In 1867 he married his second wife, Anna Snitkina, and found in her a faithful companion who gradually helped him to pay his debts and even to achieve financial stability. He had four children, but two of them died in infancy.

The last period of his life, from 1872–81, was a time of peace and popularity. Dostoevsky's fame spread all over Russia. A publication called *The Journal of an Author*, which he started in 1873 and continued at intervals until his death, was widely read and provided him with a platform from which he could preach his political and philosophical ideas.

The last and greatest of his novels, *The Brothers Karamazov*, published in 1879–80, was at once recognised as a work of genius. Dostoevsky was no longer treated as a mere novelist. He had become a teacher of life. His famous Pushkin speech, delivered in 1880, six months before his death, raised him to the height of his fame. This oration was greeted by friend and foe as a prophetic description of Russia's destiny. To the same period of his life belonged his friendship with Vladimir Soloviev (1853–1900), who profoundly impressed Dostoevsky and was also deeply influenced by him. With Soloviev Dostoevsky in 1879 visited Optina Pustyn, one of the great centres of Russian monasticism, and this pilgrimage was an expression of their love and veneration for the Orthodox Church.

Dostoevsky had never been strong, and his letters even before his exile to Siberia contain frequent references to his bad health. As the result of his imprisonment, he developed epilepsy, from which he suffered acutely till the end of his life. His physical infirmities, his over-sensibility and his constant financial worries often made literary work an agony to him, but nothing could stop him from writing, and his desire to create triumphed over all obstacles. He died after a short illness on January 28th, 1881. His funeral was the occasion of spontaneous manifestations of popular grief. No Russian writer was more lamented than Dostoevsky, though his faith in the truth of Christianity was the exception rather than the rule in Russian society. He was practically unknown outside his country during his lifetime and his fame began to spread in the Western world only in the twentieth century.

There are several descriptions of Dostoevsky made by his contemporaries. None of them are neutral. He was either admired or attacked.

He was a typical Russian in appearance: he might be taken for an ordinary peasant, but his broad forehead proclaimed his exceptional intellectual gifts, and the expression of his eyes revealed an experience of great suffering and an unusual knowledge of life.

All his writings can be treated as an autobiography, for his heroes debate the problems which preoccupied his mind and live through the passions, fears and hopes so familiar to Dostoevsky himself. But he saw himself with such lucidity that his novels became, like the Greek classical tragedies, monuments of the eternal drama of the human spirit.

Dostoevsky was a person of many dimensions, and so are his writings. They are first of all the narrative of his own life, but he liked to present it under the form of a detective story. They are a masterly analysis of the nineteenth-century man caught in the crisis of humanism, but this particular stage in the European civilisation was used by him as an illustration of the great theological theme: the creature confronting its Creator. Finally, his writings are strongly coloured by political journalism, but their inspiration comes from the insight of a prophet.

All his life Dostoevsky was absorbed in the solution of a single problem. His lifelong passion was the study of man, and his contributions in this field completely revolutionised modern psychology and sociology. Dostoevsky can be described as a person who suddenly discovers in a well-known building a number of rooms, passages and cellars, the very existence of which is unsuspected by the owners of the house. He was able to penetrate those concealed corners of the human soul which had not been visited before by scholars and writers.

Dostoevsky's man, compared with man as he appears in the works of other authors, seems to possess a fourth dimension. He is infinitely more perturbing and irrational than the human beings conventionally presented before Dostoevsky's time. His men no longer fit into the familiar categories of positive and negative characters. It is impossible to call them intelligent or stupid, moral or immoral, even good or bad. They are capable of heroism and self-sacrifice, and at the same time they can commit vile and cruel deeds. They stand on the edge of a precipice of crime and degradation, and yet they long for goodness and truth. Their whole life is a struggle; they are torn between their hopes and fears. Love and hate, a readiness to help and a desire to hurt constantly contest in them, so that no one can predict which tendency will eventually win and in which direction they will move. At first sight, men as seen by Dostoevsky appear to be grotesque, abnormal beings; one is inclined to dismiss them as pathological cases, as the creation of the unbalanced mind of that strange author. But this first impression disappears when they are more carefully analysed. One can see then that their problems and struggle are typical of those which beset all human beings, that the impression of unreality first produced is due to the concentration in a short space of time, of a conflict which is usually spread over many years in the life of other people. Dostoevsky's writings break new ground because he faces boldly and frankly those conflicts which men usually keep secret even from their closest friends.

His novels show man in all his perplexity and contradictions, and disclose a power of good and evil such as most men are seldom ready to acknowledge in themselves.

Dostoevsky is rightly described as a writer who discovered the existence of the underworld in every human being and explained the significance of the subconscious and irrational. Whether one likes or deplores his picture of man, one has to recognise that his writings mark a turning point in the history of modern civilisation. He brought to an end that optimistic humanism which closed its eyes to the dark explosive elements of human nature and represented man as a rational, straightforward creature, who could reach a higher stage of progress as the result of better education and more satisfactory social and economic conditions. Dostoevsky gave the death-blow to this outlook which had inspired Europe from the time of the Renaissance till the first decade of the twentieth century.

He is therefore a true interpreter of the present troubled and restless epoch. The study of the underworld was not, however, his only achievement. The more he penetrated into the innermost chambers of the human soul, the more captivated he was by the mystery of man and by the opposing tendencies of his nature. The greatest of Dostoevsky's discoveries was that man could not be explained in purely human terms, that in him was contained the secret of the whole universe, and in him lay its final revelation.

Dostoevsky's analysis of the conflict between good and evil led him to the conclusion that both these forces originated outside human beings, that they were more powerful than man himself.

Man was not the author either of good or evil, but he was the field of their never-ceasing struggle. Dostoevsky taught that man in his ascent towards goodness could reach heights surpassing man's own picture of perfection and in his degradation he could descend into an abyss of evil which terrified even its own victims. He firmly believed that personality is the highest manifestation of life and that therefore good and evil outside man have also personal existence. In other words, he asserted the traditional Christian belief that man's place was between God and Satan.

Such a definition of man recalls the mediæval pictures representing human beings assaulted by hordes of devils and protected by angels. Dostoevsky would not dismiss these pictures as altogether childish and naïve, as most of his contemporaries brought up in the atmosphere of Western civilisation were inclined to do. He was too well aware of the essential mystery of man to treat this age-long interpretation of human destiny lightly. Yet his conception differed from the mediæval one, for it asserted with hitherto unknown emphasis the absolute freedom of man to make a choice between good and evil, to take God's side or Satan's. According to Dostoevsky, man was much more free than most men knew themselves to be; he was surprisingly, staggeringly free; he could resist God to the very end, and there was no power on earth or in heaven which could break down man's independence and destroy the freedom of this strange and in other respects weak creature. Father Zossima, in *The Brothers Karamazov*, expresses this conviction when he says: "Oh, there are some who remain proud and fierce even in hell in spite of their certain knowledge and contemplation of the absolute truth. . . . They refuse forgiveness, they curse God who calls them. They cannot behold the Living God without hatred, and they cry out that the God of Life should be annihilated: that God should destroy Himself and His own creation. And they will burn in the fire of their own wrath for ever, and yearn for death and annihilation, but they will not attain to death."

There is one thing, however, that a human being does not possess, and that is the power to destroy himself, for if he could do it he would be stronger than the Creator Himself, but man can refuse co-operation with God; he is free, as Ivan Karamazov says, "respect-fully to return the ticket to God." The stage set for man fails to satisfy him. He feels bored and disgruntled. He is convinced that, left to himself, he could manage things much better. He can leave the stage and go away; no one will stop him, for he is truly his own master. But his act of protest and self-will provokes in man an inner insoluble conflict.

Dostoevsky discussed the nature of man's freedom in all his main novels. Especially in the person of Kirilov in *The Possessed*, he studied all the stages of man's rebellion against his Creator. His conclusion was that, having freed himself from belief in God, man was bound to deify himself, to put himself above all moral laws, to proclaim that everything was permissible, for if God did not exist then man was the lord of creation. This assertion of his own absolute freedom brought man face to face with the presence in his soul of dark and irrational forces which dragged man from his high pedestal and enslaved him by establishing their iron control over his personality. As soon as man declared that everything was lawful he became a helpless victim of his own passions, fears and doubts. He found himself in the clutch of his impotence and corruption, and the only act left to his freedom was suicide.

This was the final conclusion reached by Kirilov, who declared: "God is nothing else than pain and fear of death. He who conquers suffering and fear of death will become God Himself. Then there will be new life, a new man . . . everything will be renewed. The whole of history is divided into two parts, the first from the gorilla to the destruction of God, the second from the destruction of God to the change of the earth and of man. Everyone who wants to attain complete freedom must be daring enough to kill himself. . . . This is the final limit of freedom, this is all, there is nothing beyond it. Who dares to kill himself becomes God. Everyone can do this and thus cause God to cease to exist, and then nothing will exist at all. But this has never yet been done and therefore the world continues to be." Kirilov is firmly convinced that if God and life eternal are only the fruits of man's imagination, by committing suicide man achieves, not only final self-annihilation, but he also destroys the whole universe. Thus the same man who proudly claims that he can stage a better production than God ends with the decision to smash up everything; his desire for self-sufficiency leads him to self-destruction. What then is the cause of man's dissatisfaction? Why is life as he sees it around him not according to his taste?

Dostoevsky's answer was that man could not reconcile himself to the present state of the world because of suffering. He could not feel happy as long as his every step was threatened by fear of pain and death.

Dostoevsky spent his childhood on the premises of a big hospital in Moscow, where his father, as a doctor, had a modest apartment. He was therefore familiar from the start of his life with the sight of poverty and disease. Already his first novel reveals his extraordinary sensitiveness to every kind of suffering. Four years of hard labour in Siberia gave him another and this time almost unique opportunity of studying all forms of mental and bodily torment and of experiencing many of them personally. He can therefore be called an expert in suffering. All his life he searched for the answer to this greatest problem of human life, and no one raised with greater boldness the question whether the Christian belief in the God of love can be reconciled with the bitter sufferings which form such an important part of man's life.

Dostoevsky faced the problem of pain in its full, naked horror. He was singularly free from any naïve illusions that suffering can be eliminated by education or better social conditions, or that it can be explained away as a temporary stage caused by poverty or bad upbringing. He knew only too well that a healthy and intelligent man might sometimes have an irresistible longing to torture other human beings, weaker and more helpless than himself, that he could enjoy the sufferings of his victims, laugh at the sight of their agony, and remain unperturbed, like the red-cheeked officer in the Siberian prison who experienced such delight at the execution of convicts beaten to death by the sticks of the soldiers. Dostoevsky was one of the few writers who observed at close quarters the mentality and psychology of executioners. The lines written by him on this subject in *The House of the Dead* deserve careful study. He said: "There are people who, like tigers, are greedy for blood. Those who have possessed unlimited power over the flesh, blood and soul of their fellow creatures, of their brethren—according to the law of Christ—those who have possessed this power and who have been able to degrade with a supreme degradation another being made in the image of God, these men are incapable of resisting their desires and their thirst for sensations. . . . I declare that the best man in the world can become hardened and brutalised to such a point that nothing will distinguish him from a wild beast."

Dostoevsky states: "Many times I have met the executioners. They all were well-developed men with common sense and intelligence, but also with inordinate self-love and even pride." He was far from treating these men as monsters. He believed that the qualities which make an executioner were potentially present in almost every modern man, and were more accentuated in him than in simpler and less educated people. Dostoevsky's description of the mentality of convicts, murderers and torturers of small children was equally challenging. He realised that many of them would again commit the same crimes in full use of their mental faculties if they had another chance of doing so. He knew the depth of suffering which one man could inflict upon another, and also the inner torture which the same man could experience as the result of his willing submission to the powers of darkness. Dostoevsky was not dismayed by the appalling spectacle of human degradation, for he found the answer to the problem of evil and pain. They were for him the price paid by men for the gift of their freedom. It was the final and complete proof of their responsibilty and independence. God truly left human beings to choose their own ways of life; He would not interfere with their moral freedom, and treated them, not like small children or slaves, but as His friends and equals who could either stay in His mansions or leave them and dwell in their own camp. But those who went away had to suffer, for they deprived themselves of the only source of happiness and life. Dostoevsky discovered the paradox of the co-existence in men's hearts of intense fear of suffering, and of readiness for it. Man, according to him, was prepared at first to sell his freedom in the hope of escaping suffering, but once he became a slave he revolted against his captivity and was ready to plunge back into the ocean of struggle and affliction in order to regain his freedom. There was nothing that men loved more than their liberty, the sense that they could do what they liked even if it was absurd, painful and destructive. There is a passage in *Letters from the Underworld* which expresses in a most striking manner this irrational and irresistible longing of man to follow his own desire, however extravagant this may be. The hero of these letters describes the state of perfect harmony and reasonableness reached by mankind after much effort and sacrifice, and then he says: "I should not be surprised if amidst all this order and regularity of the future there should suddenly arise some common-faced or rather cynical and sneering gentleman who, with his arms akimbo, will say to us: 'Now then, you fellows, what about smashing all this order to bits, sending their logarithms to the devil and living according to our own silly will.' That might not be much, but the annoying thing is that he would immediately get plenty of followers." Later comes the following passage: "Where then have all these wiseacres found that man's will should primarily be normal and virtuous? Why have they imagined that man needs a will directed towards reason and his own benefit? All he needs is an independent will, whatever it may cost him, and wherever it may lead him. . . . And why are you gentlemen so firmly and solemnly convinced that only that which is normal and positive, in a word, his well-being, is good for man? Is the reason never deceived about what is beneficial? Isn't it possible that as well as loving his own welfare, man is fond of suffering, even passionately fond of it. . . . I am sure that man will never renounce genuine suffering even if it brings ruin and chaos. Why, suffering is the one and only source of true knowledge; adversity is the mainspring of self-realisation." Dostoevsky shows that suffering lies in the very nature of man as a free and morally responsible being, that nothing can eliminate it as long as man remains what he is, and that the purpose of human evolution is not to abolish suffering, but to explain its meaning, for only those who are not afraid of pain are matured and truly free people.

Man was a microcosm for Dostoevsky. All problems, religious, political and economic, according to him, had their origin and their solution in human personality. The conflicts and tensions experienced by an individual were the pattern of wider clashes, social and even cosmic. The fear of suffering, the revolt against freedom, coupled with the attraction for both of them, were for Dostoevsky the main driving forces behind history. Especially the events of his own time he interpreted as heralding the last and most decisive stage in this drama of man. He can be called the prophet of totalitarianism. With surprising accuracy, he described the mentality of the leaders of the great social and religious revolutions of the twentieth century. He could do it because he understood the inner causes of the approaching upheaval. Dostoevsky was not a reactionary in politics, and especially in social matters he was uncompromisingly hostile to the egoistic, self-satisfied capitalistic world of his own day. He was an advocate of social and economic justice, and was ready to bear any personal sacrifice for the sake of the poor and downtrodden. And yet, in spite of his insistence on the urgent need of social improvements, he was the greatest enemy of the coming Revolution, the advent of which he so clearly foresaw. The reason for his opposition was his belief that the movement for social reform was inspired and controlled

G

by men who were rebels against God, and who therefore, far from leading men into the Promised Land, would drag them into a state of slavery and oppression.

There is no evidence that Dostoevsky was acquainted with Karl Marx's teaching, but he was familiar with the ideas of the early French Socialists, and he detected in their writings the belief which received such powerful expression in the works both of the founder of modern Communism and of Marx's disciple, Lenin—namely, that the only way to a perfect social order is through the blood and toil of world-wide revolution.

Dostoevsky discovered the deep-seated religious motives behind the coming rebellion, and he defined it as a collective expression of the same refusal to play the game according to God's rules, which he so often described as the cause of the inner disintegration of an individual. Beneath the ardent longing of the revolutionaries to assist the poor, to destroy the power of the rich, and to establish equality and justice, he saw another and even stronger desire to rearrange the world according to their own will, to dethrone the Creator, and to prove that emancipated man can be the master of his own destiny.

In support of this statement, Dostoevsky produced a number of active revolutionaries among his heroes, and they are some of the most striking personalities he created. He presented these benefactors of mankind as men who profoundly despised those common people for the sake of whose liberation they were ready to sacrifice their own life as well as the lives of others.

The Grand Inquisitor of *The Brothers Karamazov*, the great philanthropist who accused Christ of a lack of love for weak and fallible man, and who reproached the Saviour for imposing too heavy a burden of freedom upon those who could not bear it, says to his Divine Prisoner: "We have vanquished freedom, and have done so to make men happy . . . not those few who can follow Thee, . . . but those tens of thousands of millions who will not have the strength to forgo the earthly bread for the sake of the heavenly."

The Grand Inquisitor continues: "No science will give men bread so long as they remain free, they will understand themselves that freedom and bread enough for all are inconceivable together, for never, never will they be able to share between them. They will be convinced that they can never be free, for they are vicious, worthless and rebellious." With the foresight of a genius, Dostoevsky detected in the soul of the revolutionary leaders the co-existence of a genuine desire to help the oppressed and ignorant, and an equally strong disgust at the sight of the stupidity and selfishness of their fellow people. The instigators of the approaching Revolution hated God and despised man—His creation; they were convinced that they alone knew the truth, that the common man, left to himself, would always act like a fool or a knave, and therefore they were determined to use every form of compulsion and deceit in order to force men to take the road which would lead them to the earthly paradise of their own making. They asserted that as God has failed to create a world satisfying to men, they had to rebuild it on a new plan, for they possessed the secret of universal happiness, which would illuminate for ever suffering and also freedom.

Dostoevsky, with uncanny perception, was able to see the secret motives behind their actions; he expressed aloud their thoughts concealed even from themselves; he developed the ideas which they kept locked in the chambers of their subconscious self. His disclosures created an outburst of indignant protest among the enthusiasts for revolutionary action, but when totalitarianism was established at last, its leaders behaved exactly in the way predicted by Dostoevsky.

Shchigalov, for instance, in *The Possessed*, develops his theory that absolute freedom in the atheistic state of the future will lead inevitably to absolute despotism. He described how every member of collective society will be ordered to spy over all the others, and to denounce the guilty to the Government, how everyone will belong to all, and all to everyone.

Another prophetic figure created by Dostoevsky was Peter Verkhovensky from the same novel, *The Possessed*. He is the master of conspiracy and propaganda and would make an ideal Chief of Police under a totalitarian system. He suggests, for instance, that in order to overcome the feeling of boredom inevitable in the collective society, where individual freedom is radically suppressed, the rulers of the future will be obliged to encourage, from time to time, a massacre of one group by the citizens of the others, an idea which has received such a wide application in the modern world in the form of State-sponsored destruction of class or racial enemies.

Verkhovensky seemed a moral monster in the liberal and easy-going atmosphere of the nineteenth century, but he has become a familiar figure among the leading officials of totalitarian States. He is cruel and cynical; he believes that only the lowest motives of fear, greed and envy can influence men and rouse them to action. He tries to secure control over his followers by forcing them to commit crimes, but he himself has a deep-seated longing to submit his will to a leader who has faith, nobility and strength. He simultaneously worships and hates his idol, Stavrogin; he is ready to destroy anyone if ordered to do so by his superman, but he will be the first to avenge his disillusionment with his *Führer* if he finds in him a sign of indecision or fear.

The new world of the self-sufficiency of man was for Dostoevsky a state of "indescribable darkness and horror prepared for mankind under the disguise of renovation and resurrection."[1] He foresaw that the leaders of the coming rebellion against God would use every weapon at their disposal to establish their control over the masses; that they would give promises which they knew they could never fulfil and encourage the lowest passions and instincts, thus preparing the way for their own triumph. Dostoevsky actually anticipated some of the slogans of the atheistic revolution—for example, Lenin's famous appeal to the masses to rob the robbers or, in other words, to start universal plunder, justifying it on the ground that all the possessions of the well-to-do had been acquired through previous acts of exploitation. This order, emanating from the new leader of the State, plunged the country into anarchy and confusion, and greatly facilitated the establishment of Lenin's dictatorship.[2]

Dostoevsky was so familiar with the psychology of the men and women working for totalitarianism that he was able to forecast all the steps which they would take on their road to victory. He was equally accurate in his prediction as to the time of the coming clash. In the May-June issue of the *Journal of an Author* for the year 1877, he wrote: "It seems to me this century will end for old Europe with something colossal, I mean with something, if not exactly like the events of the French Revolution of the eighteenth century, yet nevertheless so colossal, so irresistible and terrifying that it will change the face of the earth at any rate in Western Europe."

Dostoevsky's prophecy was fulfilled. The catastrophe took place fourteen years after the end of the nineteenth century, and, as he foresaw, Russia was called to take a leading role in the great crisis of European civilisation.

[1] *Journal of an Author*, No. 50, 1873.   [2] Ibid.

Dostoevsky's roots were in the nineteenth century, and he was a contemporary of the Slavophils and of the Westernisers. Conservatism, liberalism and radicalism were the political realities of his day, but he himself belonged to another world. His face was turned towards the future, and in all his writings he discussed events which had yet to come. He was so certain about the inevitability of changes, and of their direction, that his valuation of the political and social movements of his own time was strongly coloured by this knowledge. He appeared, therefore, a puzzling and irritating figure to the men of his generation who lacked his foresight and were unable to follow the trend of his thought. His attitude to Russia was particularly disconcerting, for he could not be identified with either the Slavophils or the Westernisers. Dostoevsky often called himself a Slavophil, and he shared their fundamental conviction that the Russians were called to redeem Europe from the selfishness and scepticism which undermined her vitality. He believed as they did that the world-wide significance of the Russian people was based, not on their racial qualities, but on the superiority of the Orthodox interpretation of Christianity over that of Rome or of Protestantism. He could not, however, agree with the hostile attitude of their party towards Peter the Great, whom Dostoevsky ardently admired. He considered him to be one of the greatest Russians, one who opened a new horizon to the nation and prepared it for its world-wide mission. His wholehearted acceptance of Peter's reforms brought him almost into line with the Westernisers, but he sharply attacked them for their uncritical imitation of the West, and for their lack of understanding of the importance of religion.

A belief in the special mission of one's own nation is often accompanied by intolerance and a dislike of other people. Dostoevsky was free from these psychological dangers. He loved Europe, and, like all other educated Russians of the nineteenth century, he considered himself and his own country to be an integral part of Western civilisation. In the *Journal of an Author*, January, 1877, published during the Russian-Turkish War, when all Western nations were hostile or suspicious of the Russian desire to liberate the Balkan Christians from the Mahometan yoke, he wrote: "We cannot separate ourselves from Europe. Europe is our second home. I am the first to confess it with all my passion, and I always have done so. Europe is almost as dear to all of us as is Russia herself. Europe contains all the Aryan people, and our ideal is the unity of all these nations, and even a much wider union which shall include the Semitic and coloured peoples."

Dostoevsky was disgusted by the cult of egoism among individuals, and nations in the West; he deplored the exclusive preoccupation with material comfort, and the aquisition of wealth among the European people, but his anger was caused by his love of the West, by his firm trust that a better course was still open to its citizens.

"Europe! What an inspiring and sacred thing Europe is! Do you know, gentlemen, how dear this same Europe is to us—the dreamers, the Slavophils, who are, according to you, the haters of Europe? She is to us the land of 'sacred wonders'. Do you know how we love and venerate the great nations inhabiting her, and all their outstanding and noble achievements? Do you know how tormented and worried we are by the fate of this dear native land of ours, how frightened we are by the sinister clouds which more and more envelop her horizon? Never have you gentlemen, Westernisers and Europeans, loved Europe as much as we love her—we, the Slavophils, who, according to you, are her greatest enemies" (*Journal of an Author*, July-August, 1877).

Dostoevsky did not, however, believe that Europe could be saved from disaster by her own resources. His pessimism was due to a profound mistrust of the two great spiritual forces which have for centuries contested for dominion over her people. These were Rome, together with her often disobedient but still devout daughter, France, and their implacable enemy, the Germans. Dostoevsky disliked the spirit of Rome. He associated it with denial of freedom, lust for power and readiness to compromise with evil if such a compromise promised immediate advantages. There is no evidence that he ever met the other side of the Roman Church— her saints, mystics and missionaries. Dostoevsky's eyes were fixed on the worldly façade of the majestic Roman edifice, and he rejected it as anti-Christian. He proclaimed that the revolt against God and freedom as manifested in Europe had its deep roots in the Roman system demanding submission to authority even when such an obedience conflicts with the voice of conscience. Several times he expressed his conviction that there was a possibility of a working compromise between the Vatican and totalitarianism.

In the May–June *Journal of an Author* for 1877, Dostoevsky wrote: "Socialism is the coming power for the whole of Western Europe. If at some time in the future the Popes find themselves abandoned by the governments of this world, then it is quite possible that they will throw in their lot with a Godless Socialism.

The Pope will appear before the multitude as a barefooted beggar, and will declare that all the Socialists want and teach is in the Gospel, but that not till this moment has it been opportune to make such a disclosure." Dostoevsky was particularly interested in the destiny of France. He considered her to be the most accomplished product of the Roman interpretation of Christianity. The spirit of the French *bourgeoisie*, with its narrow selfishness and opportunism, as well as the growing force of French Socialism, with its irreligion, both seemed to him to be the ugly fruits of a defective understanding of what true Christianity is. He felt that religion conceived in terms of external authority, obedience and discipline, was separated only by one step from atheism. He claimed that the godless collectivism of the Socialists was a child of the order that professed belief in God, but lacked respect for the freedom and responsibility of men.

Besides Rome there was, however, according to Dostoevsky, another Power in Europe—namely, Germany—which was implacably bent on opposing all Roman tradition. "Germany's role is always the same. This is to protest," wrote Dostoevsky in the May–June, 1877, *Journal*. "Ancient Rome was the first to bestow upon mankind the idea of universal unity, and she firmly believed that she could achieve it under the form of universal monarchy. This form collapsed, however, under the Christian pressure, but the idea itself survived and is still the living heart of European civilisation."

"The proud and powerful German people, from the very beginning of their history, could never agree to co-operate in this task. They fought first in battles against the Roman legions, then at the time of the Reformation they split asunder the spiritual unity of Western Christendom, and they are still opposed to all European nations which have inherited the Roman ideal."

Dostoevsky realised that Germany would try to establish her own pattern of unity in Europe, but at the same time he thought that the Germans lacked constructive ideas, and therefore their undying opposition to Roman universalism was fundamentally destructive. If they succeeded in crushing their enemy, they would feel lost for they had nothing positive to offer (*Journal of an Author*, May–June, 1877).

Neither Rome, with her scheme of compulsory unity, nor Germany, with her Protestantism, could therefore save Europe, and establish mutual understanding and co-operation among the nations. This vital task, according to Dostoevsky, could be achieved only by the Russian people. A large part of the *Journal of an Author* was dedicated by him to the elaboration of this central idea of his whole philosophy of life. A few months before his death in August, 1880, he went back to it once more. He wrote: "The Russian soul, the genius of the Russian people, is more capable than any other nation of incorporating the idea of universal unity, of brotherly love and of realistic outlook, forgiving those who are hostile, discriminating, understanding those who differ, and solving contradictions."

In his famous Pushkin speech, made in Moscow on June 8th, 1880, Dostoevsky described this greatest of the Russian poets as a prophetic symbol of the whole Russian nation, for Pushkin possessed the unique gift of identifying himself with different nations of Europe and Asia, and of expressing their thoughts and feelings in the way most typical of them.

This universalism of the Russian nation was rooted, according to Dostoevsky, in another characteristic of Russian mentality— freedom from fear of suffering. The Russians were not afraid to suffer because they understood the meaning of pain. They accepted the necessity of this hardest of all trials, for it secured the growth and maturity of personality.

Dostoevsky insisted that the Russians could even welcome and love suffering. He wrote:[1] "I think that the main, the fundamental spiritual necessity of the Russian people is the need of suffering, of constant, ubiquitous suffering. It seems that we have felt that need from time immemorial. The Russian people even in their happiness experience some degree of pain, otherwise their happiness lacks its fullness. Never even in the most triumphant moments of their history were the Russian people proud or arrogant. On the contrary, they remained humble and penitent, ascribing their victory, not to their own efforts, but to God's gracious help and protection." This nearness to suffering, the readiness to welcome it, coupled with humility and the realisation of man's dependence on God, were, according to Dostoevsky, those characteristics of the Russian people which enabled them to enter into a close fellowship with other nations. Their hearts and minds were open to the flow of new life coming from others. They possessed that facility to understand others which is only given to those who have suffered much and yet are not hardened and embittered by their experience.

[1] *Journal of an Author*, No. 4, 1873.

Dostoevsky did not claim that Russian people have succeeded in fulfilling their mission. He believed, however, that the school of long suffering and privation had so well prepared the ground for action that the day would come when Russia would lead the rest of the world in the building up of a genuine Christian order.

"We shall see," wrote Dostoevsky, in the January, 1877, issue of the *Journal of an Author*, "that the bearers of true Socialism are none other than our common Russian people, that their spirit contains a living desire of all-embracing unity for the entire human race, a unity with complete respect for national individuality and with careful preservation of freedom for all men. This unity consists of love and service, and is based on the actual realisation of brotherhood and not on cutting off millions of human heads."

In his Pushkin speech, Dostoevsky proclaimed: "For a true Russian, Europe and her destiny are as dear as the fate of her own land, because our destiny is universality, acquired not by the sword but by the strength of brotherhood, and by our desire to see the restoration of concord among all men."

He developed at greater length the same idea in his last issue of the *Journal of an Author*, published in 1881: "Our people, in the overwhelming majority, are still Orthodox, and they live by this ideal, though they do not express their ideal in a rational and scientific manner. As a matter of fact, our people have nothing else to offer except this ideal. They sincerely desire to build their whole life upon this foundation, though often they pollute themselves by sin and become pitiful victims of their ignorance and passions. . . . The main mistake of the Russian intelligentsia is that they do not recognise the presence of the Church among the Russian people. I do not speak now about the church buildings or clergy; I speak about our Russian Socialism—the aim of which is the realisation of a universal Church on earth in the degree in which the earth can embrace the fullness of the Church. I speak about the never-quenched, ever-present thirst among Russian people for the great universal and brotherly oneness in the name of Christ. . . . Not in Communism, not in its mechanical forms, is contained the Socialism of the Russian people. They believe that the final salvation and the all-illuminating unity is in Christ and in Him alone. This is our Russian Socialism. Those who do not understand the meaning of Orthodoxy for our common people, and its final purpose, will never be able to understand our nation." Dostoevsky opposed Russian Socialism to Western Communism on the ground that the West seeks salvation through the perfection of the outward forms of organisation, whilst the only real transforming power lies in the Personality of Christ, the Saviour of the world.

"The Roman Empire incorporated the moral efforts of the whole ancient world: her religious ideal was man-god, but she could not realise it, for her strength was undermined by the growing power of the Church. A clash occurred between these two opposite ideals. Man-god encountered God-man, Apollo met Christ. The result was a compromise: the Empire accepted Christianity, and the Church blessed Roman law and Roman State. A small section of the Church retired into the desert and continued there its previous work through its religious communities, but these were isolated experiments, and the same situation has lasted till our day. Meanwhile, the major part of the Church became split into the Western and the Eastern parts. In the West the State conquered the Church. Papacy is the continuation of the ancient Roman Empire under a new form. In the East the State was destroyed and dissolved by the Mohametans, but Christ remained there though isolated from the State. In Russia the State accepted Christ, but, owing to the Tartars and many external calamities and internal disorders, the proper form of the Christian social order has not yet been produced. The Russian people, however, bear the image of Christ and love Him only" (*Journal of an Author*, 1881).

Such a philosophy of history may give an impression of undue simplification of its complex problems. Dostoevsky seems to find the solution of every personal and social conflict in the meeting between the individual and Christ, and his opponents accused him of pietism, of under-estimation of the importance of better education and of the urgent need of economic improvements.

Dostoevsky was not a pietist; nothing was farther removed from his mind than a desire to identify the task of Christianity with the salvation of individual souls. He was vitally concerned with the social implication of religion, and he professed a belief in the world-wide mission of Russian Christians,[1] but he interpreted this mission as the revelation of the true meaning of the Church to the rest of mankind.

[1] "Every great nation, if it wants to survive, must believe that in it and in it alone lies the salvation of the world, and its purpose is to lead in harmony all the nations towards the final goal of their common destiny" (*Journal of an Author*, January, 1877).

He called himself a Christian Socialist, for he knew by experience that a genuine conversion radically altered the attitude of a man to his neighbours. A religion without social implications, a Christian who remained egocentric, were to him contradictions in terms, for the first-fruit of Christian regeneration was the realisation of the unity and interdependence of all men. Those who did not recognise Christ in their neighbour had never met their Saviour. Dostoevsky looked forward to a time when the State would be dissolved in the brotherhood of the Church, when free theocracy would replace fear and compulsion, but he was certain that this perfect social order could never be achieved by unaided human efforts, let alone by the blood and destruction of class struggle. The atheists and the agnostics were to him blind leaders of the blind. The only true progress was in the experience of a new life in Christ.

The cure for social evil proposed by Dostoevsky is bound to disappoint many of his readers, for it appears to have nothing new about it. It is as old as Christianity itself. Dostoevsky seems to lack originality here, for he follows closely the thought expressed in St. John's Gospel and Epistles. This is however precisely his great contribution, for there is unquestionably a special significance in the fact that the most outstanding student of psychology in the nineteenth century arrived at the same conclusions as those reached by the seer of the first century. Dostoevsky and St. John belonged to two different worlds; their outlook and background were entirely different, yet their approach to the mystery of man was the same. This cannot be ascribed to mere coincidence. Their agreement signifies that they were able to unlock some of the greatest secrets of human nature.

Dostoevsky's conviction of the universality and spiritual maturity of the Russian people, of their firm grasp of the unity and interdependence of all nations, can easily appear extravagant and arbitrary, an expression of his national pride and wishful thinking. But he was not addicted to the cult of nationalism. He ascribed the gifts possessed by the Russian people, not to their superior natural qualities, which he denied, but to their personal meeting with Christ, which transformed and elevated the whole nation.

Dostoevsky was aware how such a statement would shock both the Western world and those Russians who were brought up in its traditions. In the eyes of Europe, the majority of Russians were barbarians who had neither culture nor learning. They were illiterate peasants, given to drunkenness and other forms of intemperance, poor and oppressed, leading an almost animal state of existence. Dostoevsky knew how deeply rooted were these misconceptions, and he wages a never-ceasing war against these false notions. His insistence that a real knowledge of Christ existed among the Russian common people[1] was based on his hard experience of four long years spent with the Russian convicts in Siberia.

Dostoevsky was a member of the educated Russian class. As a youth he mixed more than others of his kind with the common people, and the deeply-moving story of his encounter with a peasant called Marey (*Journal of an Author*, February, 1876) at the age of nine shows how lively were his early contacts with peasants. But it was only when he was forced to live their life, when he was stripped of all his social privileges, that he learned to see them in their true light. He wrote (*Journal of an Author*, No. 50, 1873): "I became one of them. I stood on their level. I was even put on the lowest of all social levels." He had no illusions about the sins and failures of the Russian people. He saw the most brutal and repulsive side of their character, and not as a detached observer, but as a victim of their cruelty. In his *Journal of an Author* (1880) he wrote: "Yes, our common people are rough, but not all of them, and I can say this as a witness, for I lived with common people for years. I know them, I ate with them, slept with them, I was myself counted as one of their outcasts. I worked with them, their own hard labour. . . . Don't tell me, please, therefore, that I have no knowledge of Russian peasants."

This meeting with the Russian masses was a turning point in his life. It reorientated the whole course of his existence and opened up a new and hitherto unknown world to Dostoevsky. The first thing which struck him profoundly and painfully was the gulf which separated him from the bulk of the Russian people. Only in Siberia did he realise how utterly alien were the educated Russians to their own people. They belonged to two different worlds, and the common language between them was lost. The second discovery made by him was that the Russian peasants were

[1] Anatole Leroy-Beaulieu, a famous French historian, the best authority on Russia of the nineteenth century, in his well-known study, *L'Empire des Tzars* (Paris, 1889), corroborates Dostoevsky's assertion. He writes: "The Russian peasant is almost alone in Europe in his search for the pearl of the Gospel parable, and he venerates the hands which have found it. He still loves the Cross, and this is the essence of Christianity, and he still accepts the virtue of suffering" (Vol. III, pp. 44–5).

far from being savages. They were bearers of a vigorous and
original culture of their own, which contained treasures unknown
to Western Europe and to those Russians who were brought up
in its tradition. The *Journal of an Author* contains Dostoevsky's
constant appeals to the Russian intelligentsia to start learning from
the common people, to stop looking down upon them as uncouth
and undeveloped.

The surprising element in this discovery was that Dostoevsky
did not meet the best of the Russian peasants. On the contrary, he
lived among criminals, but even they, as members of the peasant
community, were able to explain to him things which he did not
realise before. They were crude and desperate men; many of them
were heavily burdened by their crimes, and yet they still shared
that sound knowledge of God and man which was the great
achievement of the old Russian culture, and which Dostoevsky—
a leading representative of the Westernised intellectual circles of
the capital—was to learn from them. Their outlook was sound,
for it was built on a solid foundation, on the Gospel of Christ as
interpreted by the Eucharist of the Eastern Orthodox Church.
"The Russian people know Christ in their heart, and possess His
true image. It has been handed down to them from one generation
to another, and now is deeply planted in their hearts. It is possible
that Christ is the only true love of the Russian nation, and they
love Him in their own typical way, they love Him and suffer
because of their sins" (*Journal of an Author*, No. 4, 1873).

Dostoevsky learned to respect Russian peasants, to admire their
deep sense of justice, their courage and patience, their humility and
realism, and, above all, their sound scale of values. Many of those
whom he met in Siberia were morally sick people, but they knew
good and evil and had a clear idea what Christ meant to the individual and to mankind. Dostoevsky, too, realised Christ's place
in the life of men, and he learned it when he was at the bottom of
the abyss of suffering and humiliation.

Only towards the close of his life, when he stood at the threshold
of death, did Dostoevsky reveal all that he owed to the common
people. The two last issues of his *Journal of an Author*, one published
in August, 1880, and another in 1881 after his death, are of special
importance in the study of his religious convictions. In his reply
to the liberal journalist Gradovsky, Dostoevsky explained at
length his attitude to the religious state of the Russian people.
He wrote: "I assert that our nation was enlightened a long time
ago by its acceptance of Christ and His teaching. You will argue,

Mr. Gradovsky, that our common people do not know Christian doctrines, since they seldom hear sermons. This is nonsense. They know all that it is vital to know, though they may not pass an examination on the Catechism. They have learned the truth of Christianity in the Church, where for centuries they listened to the prayers and hymns, which are infinitely better than sermons. Our common people have recited these prayers since the time when they fled to the forests from the horrors of the Tartar invasion. . . . Besides, they know by heart many lives of the saints, they love narrating them and listening to them. But the most important school of Christianity through which they have passed is the centuries of manifold, never-ending sufferings they have experienced throughout their history. Abandoned by all, trodden down by all, working hard for others, our common people have remained alone with Christ, their only comforter, whom they accepted into their hearts and retained for ever. It was He who saved them from despair. My words are bound to appear to you childish, almost indecent, but I write, not in order to convince you, but because it is such a grave matter that I must write about it while I still have strength to hold my pen. . . . It is from these common people that I received Christ in my soul, Him whom I learned to know as a child, but whom I had deserted when I became a 'liberal European.' . . ."

"There is much brutality and sinfulness among our common people, but they will never confuse what is right and what is wrong. Sin is a stench, but stench will pass when the sun arises. Sin is transient. Christ is eternal. . . . Our people are subject to many sins, but they have only one idea, only one true love, and this is Christ."

Dostoevsky ends the passage by insisting that this love for Christ is not a vague aspiration, but that it is rooted in a profound experience of Him, and has therefore produced among the common people personalities of exceptional nobility and beauty. These holy men and women have remained unknown to the upper classes of Russian society, but they have been a shining light for the suffering people of Russia.

It is impossible to understand Dostoevsky's outlook without grasping the place he ascribed to Christ in the history of mankind.

Dostoevsky was not a detached scholar. His piercing analysis of the human soul and his startling predictions of the approaching crisis were those of a prophet who warns men of coming punishment and implores them to repent and give up their evil ways. He is vital for our epoch, not only because he foresaw the course of future events, but even more because he offered the remedy for its evils, and his prescription has so far received little attention. The only power which he believed could save mankind from disaster was that belonging to Christ. Millions of human beings of all nations and epochs have accepted Christ as their Teacher and Saviour. Dostoevsky was only one of many who have been captured by the Person of Jesus of Nazareth. But his interpretation of Christ bore that same mark of vigour which characterises every idea emanating from his penetrating mind.

Jesus Christ was for Dostoevsky neither a teacher of truth nor a man who appreciated beauty and had a fine perception of goodness. Christ was for him Truth, Beauty and Goodness revealing themselves to the world through perfect human nature.

Dostoevsky never used theological terms, and he never spoke about Christ's redemptive work. But his whole life was based on the experience of redemption. A man like Dostoevsky who met evil in its most appalling and devastating forms had to possess the certainty of faith of the early martyrs to speak as he spoke about the victory of good over sin and death. This triumph of love and life was revealed to him in the Person of Christ. In Christ humanity in complete freedom, having conquered the fear of suffering and pain, obedient to the Will of the Father, set forth the pattern of harmony and perfection. Those who met Him on their way and had a glimpse of His glory and beauty were new creatures. They had seen the new light, they had been brought into touch with truth and goodness, and nothing which could happen to them afterwards could deprive them of their experience. They could be thrown into the abyss of sin, suffering and pain, they could be assaulted by despair and tortured by the spirits of lust and blasphemy, but even from the bottom of hell they could cry out, "Hosanna to the Highest!" for they knew that goodness, beauty and truth did exist, and nothing could destroy their glory. Even if they themselves were deprived of the vision, they knew that it must uplift and illuminate the rest of the created world.

Dostoevsky boldly proclaimed that "beauty will save the world." The word "beauty" expressed to Dostoevsky that spontaneous revelation of new life which Christ alone could bring into the dark existence of those who had previously failed to encounter Him. Like a piece of perfect music or a picture of a great master, so Christ's Personality strikes the human soul by its harmony and beauty, and conquers without arguments and explanations; Christ saves men by the unique quality of His Life, by the love and freedom which emanate from Him.

The world's literature does not possess any picture of Christ comparable in its power to that given by Dostoevsky in *The Legend of the Grand Inquisitor*. The most remarkable feature of this legend is Christ's complete silence; throughout the whole scene He does not say a single word. It is only the Grand Inquisitor who argues, who tries to prove his case, who hates, fears and admires. Christ stands in front of him, subdued and yet triumphant, understanding all, forgiving all and yet pronouncing His final judgment.

Christ does not need to use words in order to defend truth, for He is the Truth Incarnate. He does not ask for obedience, for only those who are completely free and love Him can follow Him. This emphasis on freedom is another keynote of Dostoevsky's interpretation of Christ. Christ can be found only by those who are not afraid of freedom, and only those are free who have conquered the fear of suffering. The slowness of Christian progress, according to Dostoevsky, has been caused by the unwillingness of the members of the Church to face the challenge of freedom. Many of them have avoided meeting Christ, and tried to fill the gap by acts of charity, by missionary zeal, by learning, or by obedience to Church authority. All these virtues, laudable as they are, are of little help, for none of them can eradicate sin, and as long as man remains the helpless victim of sin he continues to be an anti-social, irrational being, full of explosive and destructive impulses. Good example and moral rules are powerless to cure men. Only Christ, freely and unconditionally accepted by a human being, can destroy evil and restore unity and brotherhood among men.

In the light of this approach to Christ, one can explain Dostoevsky's critical attitude to the Roman Church, which he believed had displayed throughout her history mistrust of freedom, and doubted man's ability to use this gift satisfactorily.

His real enemies, however, were not the papalists, but those liberal politicians and thinkers, who abused the word "freedom" by promising to secure it for their followers, but did not mention the reality of sin. Dostoevsky treated the advocates of these social and economic theories either as fools, or as deliberate liars who considered every deception lawful if it promised success in their propaganda campaign. In July–August, 1877, of *Journal of an Author*, he wrote: "It is absolutely evident that in mankind is lurking an evil much deeper than Socialist doctors suppose, that whatever the social organisation is, evil cannot be eliminated, that the human soul will remain the same, that abnormal manifestations and sin are born in it, and, finally, that the laws of the human spirit are still so little known, are still so much outside the reach of science, so mysterious, that doctors cannot be found yet to deal with them efficiently."

Dostoevsky was not a pessimist. On the contrary, together with his friend, Vladimir Soloviev, he firmly believed in the possibility of the victory of goodness and truth here on earth. He shared the conviction that the cosmos can be transfigured, evil conquered, mankind regenerated and death eliminated.

The problem of death presented a particular fascination to Dostoevsky's mind. He had an unusual experience of it. He faced it as a young man standing on the scaffold and expecting his life to end in a few moments. Several times his eyes pierced behind its veil during his frequent attacks of epilepsy. He made many attempts to convey to his readers the revelation which he received as to the nature of death. They were never very successful. Something made it impossible for him to transmit to the world the message which he himself considered of supreme importance. He could find neither the right words nor the proper form for their expression.

Prince Myshkin, in *The Idiot*, one of the spokesmen of Dostoevsky's mind, says: "I lack the right gestures. I have no sense of proportion. I use wrong words, and they do not correspond with my thoughts, and this is degrading for thought. I always fear to compromise the great idea on account of my funny appearance."

Dostoevsky himself, in one of his last letters, wrote: "I feel there is much more buried in me than I had been able to express hitherto as a writer." In another letter he stated: "I'll die without being able to pass on to others the most important part of my idea." The same feelings are expressed by many of his heroes. They seem to be unable to bear the burden of the revelation given to them.

H

They are haunted by their visions, but they are incapable of interpreting them properly, and of conveying their intuitions to the rest of the world. If they make such attempts, they look comic, like the hero of *A Queer Fellow's Dream.*

Dostoevsky's "great idea," his Christian Socialism, as he called it, was something more striking and radical than the mere political and economic reforms based on Christian principles.

He was acutely aware that only man's complete liberation from sin could satisfy the craving of the human heart for peace and happiness, and if this victory over sinful self could ever be secured, it would carry with it the conquest of death, and the restoration to the fullness of life of the past generations.

Was this a part of a Christian revelation, or a distorted Utopianism? This was the problem which Dostoevsky debated in all his chief novels, but he gave a definite answer to it only in the last and greatest of his works, *The Brothers Karamazov.*

The decisive influence upon his attitude was a manuscript which he received in 1877 from a man named Peterson. The sender did not disclose the authorship of the remarkable document, and only later on did Dostoevsky learn that the ideas which so profoundly struck him were those of the most original of all Russian thinkers, Nikolai Feodorov (1828–1903).

In his reply to Peterson, Dostoevsky wrote:[1] "Who is the philosopher whose ideas you conveyed to me? I am immensely interested in him. In essence I agree entirely with his thoughts. I read them as if they were my own. To-day I have shown the manuscript to Vladimir Soloviev, our young philosopher . . . he also agrees with the unknown thinker."

The manuscript which so profoundly stirred both Dostoevsky and Soloviev contained, among others, the following statements:[2] "We ascribe to God's thought the creation of limited beings and of their abandonment for ever to the present unsatisfactory conditions. The creation of imperfect beings does not require, however, either omnipotence or omniscience or even absolute love. . . . Nothing positive is achieved by the mere removal of immortal beings from this world which remains mortal. . . . The true task is to transform Nature in such a way as to make it instrumental in general resurrection. The Kingdom of God or Paradise must be the creation of men themselves. It can only be the fruit of their

[1] Dostoevsky's letter was published in the newspaper *Don*, No. 80, 1897.
[2] The relation between Feodorov and Dostoevsky is discussed in A. K. Gornostaev, *Paradise on Earth*, Harbin, 1929.

matured knowledge, of their deep feelings, and of their utmost energy all directed towards the fulfilment of God's Will. They can achieve it, not in their isolation, but only through their corporate efforts in their entirety. . . . Christianity is the union of the living for the resurrection of the dead; it is the fellowship in love of those who eat and drink with the purpose in view of bringing back to the sacred meal all the departed. We eat and drink in order to be able to restore to life the dead. Christ, at the time of His departure, linked together remembrance and love for Him (and this meant for all departed) with eating, with the action which gives life and strength for work. He commanded all the living to gather together round the feast of love, of love for Him and for all the departed, of a love which gives all its energy towards making it possible to see and to hear Him again together with the other departed."

"Paradise on earth is possible, but paradise in the presence of death is ridiculous and inconceivable. There is no absolute death, however, and the destruction of temporary death is the object of our human work; it is our task."

Such were some of the paradoxical ideas contained in the manuscript. Dostoevsky responded to them enthusiastically. He found in Feodorov's thought the confirmation of his hopes and intuitions, and therefore he could write to Peterson: "It is unquestionably our duty to raise our ancestors to life. The resurrection will be real, personal. The gulf separating us from the souls of our ancestors will be bridged. Those who had been defeated by death will triumph, and they will rise up, not only metaphorically in our consciousness, but actually, individually, in their bodies."

Dostoevsky, through the mouth of the dying Stepan Trofimovich in *The Possessed*, anticipated some of Feodorov's ideas. Stepan Trofimovich says: "Every minute, every moment of life must be bliss for man . . . it must be so, it must be so. It is the duty of men themselves to arrange it. This is the law, concealed, but existing certainly." Makar, in *A Raw Youth*, is preoccupied with the same burning problem: Can man find satisfaction in his life on earth? Can he overcome the power of sin and death? But it was only after his acquaintance with Feodorov's thought that Dostoevsky at last saw clearly the answer to this question. Father Zosima, in *The Brothers Karamazov*, says quite emphatically: "We do not understand that life is a paradise, for it suffices only to wish to understand it, and at once the paradise will appear in front of us in all its beauty." It is of the utmost significance that Dostoevsky ended

The Brothers Karamazov with a triumphant note of the glory and certainty of the general resurrection. " 'Karamazov,' cried Kolia, 'can it be true what's taught us in religion that we shall all rise again from the dead, and shall live and see each other again all, Iliusha, too?' 'Certainly, we shall rise again, certainly we shall see each other and shall tell each other with joy and gladness all that has happened,' Aliosha answered, half laughing, half enthusiastic.' "
And after this declaration of his faith, Aliosha took the boys to the funeral feast, confirming by this ancient Eastern custom the prophetic words of Nikolai Feodorov that the very act of eating and drinking has a sacramental meaning promising the resurrection of the dead, and urging the living to begin their work for the accomplishment of this greatest and unique task given by God to men.

Dostoevsky intended to resume the writing of *The Brothers Karamazov*. He wanted to illustrate further his belief that only the struggle against death could satisfy man's longing for corporate creative action. His own death prevented him from the realisation of this plan. He died full of forebodings that Russia, together with the rest of the world, stood on the eve of great and terrifying events, and that it was too late to stop them from coming.

"Something new is rapidly approaching all of us, and we must be ready to meet it," wrote Dostoevsky on the eve of his death (*Journal of an Author*, 1881). The changes which he predicted have taken place, the new world of totalitarianism has come into existence, but through a door which Dostoevsky apparently failed to detect. He believed that Europe would be the first to become the victim of religious and social disintegration, and that the Russian people would be called to reveal Christ to the West. In reality Russia has fallen into the hands of the atheists, but in the West Christian civilisation has not been destroyed.

The failure on Dostoevsky's part to foresee the course of events is, however, only apparent; the fact is that he is as good a guide for the study of the Communistic revolution in Russia as for the understanding of the struggle and tensions in a human soul.

Dostoevsky's main contention that the Russian people would be called to take a lead in the history of modern Christianity has been amply confirmed by the course of recent events. The Communist Revolution is not only an economic experiment; it is also one of the sharp turning points in the religious evolution of mankind. It could take place only within a spiritually-matured and intensely religious nation. The godless movement launched by the Communists, and the unflinching resistance to it, could happen only in a country where God is a reality in the daily life of the people, where Christ's teaching presents a true challenge to the human mind, where the question of man's immortality and freedom are still burning issues. Dostoevsky was the first writer to describe the outlook of the militant atheist, a man who hates God, and who treats Christ as his personal enemy. He discovered these godless fanatics among his Russian contemporaries, but he was aware that they were heralds of a new epoch when religious problems once more would rise to pre-eminence. He contrasted these ardent atheists with the type of indifferent agnostic so common among the people of Western Europe in the nineteenth century.

Dostoevsky had a clear insight into the mentality of the men who at present lead the godless movement; he forecasted that a determined and ruthless persecution of the Christians would be launched by them as soon as they seized power. The story told by him in the *Journal of an Author* (No. 4, 1873) of a young Russian peasant whose hatred of Christ was such that he fired a shot at the Eucharistic Host, shows clearly how little Christ's followers could expect mercy at the hands of this kind of enemy. But the same story also reveals the astonishing power of faith in the persecutors. They believe in God, but, being unable to love Him, they want to attack Him and to destroy all those who dare to worship Him. Dostoevsky comments on this Russian tendency to go to extremes as most illuminating. "Russian people are liable to lose all sense of proportion. They are attracted by the edge of a precipice, they like to lean over it and to look into the abyss, and sometimes to plunge into it."

"They are capable of denouncing their most sacred ideals, of blaspheming and deriding the truth which they have worshipped, and in which they still believe" (*Journal of an Author*, No. 4, 1873).

Dostoevsky was never dismayed by the sight of human depravity, or by the violence of man's rebellion against God. He knew that this revolt was coming, and he was aware that the Russians would be at the head of it. But he also knew that the same Russians would offer the strongest opposition to the forces which aim at the enslavement of men under the pretext of their liberation. He was firmly convinced that Christ would be victorious in Russia, and from there the light of a new vision of Him would spread all over the world. Russia would bring Christ back to Europe and make Him known also in Asia.

One of the most interesting features of his *Journal of an Author* is that its last chapter was devoted to the prophetic description of Russia's role in the destiny of Oriental peoples. Dostoevsky had hardly ever touched that subject before, a subject which attracted singularly little attention from the educated Russian classes in the nineteenth century. Their whole interest was centred in Europe, and they looked down upon Asia as a continent of barbarism and oppression. With a prophetic voice, Dostoevsky foretold the great changes which occurred fifty years after his death in the relations between Russia and Asia. He wrote: "It is time for us Russians to overcome the fear that we shall be called by Europe Asiatic barbarians. We have been haunted by this fear for more than two hundred years. We have paid dearly for this fear by the loss of our spiritual independence, by our mistakes in our relations with Western nations, and, finally, by our financial difficulties. It is time for us to recognise that we are not only Europeans, but also Asiatics. We have tried hard to be admitted as equals into European society. Sometimes we menaced the West with our military power and sent our armies to save the falling crowns of their kings; on other occasions we abased ourselves before Europe and assured her that we were made to serve her interests and make her happy. . . . But Europe could never allow that we could take part on the same footing as others in the building up of her civilisation. Europe considered us foreigners to her culture, and even pretenders. The reason for this is that our message to mankind is different from hers. Europe knows it, though our Russian liberals have made most strenuous efforts to convince the West that we Russians have no ideas of our own, that we can never produce them, and our role is simply to imitate Western civilisation; yet these liberals failed to impress our Western neighbours." In this last chapter of his *Journal*, when Dostoevsky once more proclaimed that the Russian people was called to take a leading role in the spiritual destiny of Europe, he declared also that before this takes place Russia would have to pass through great crises and establish a new type of relations with unknown Asia. "Our country will pass through the same transformation which was experienced by Europe at the time of the discovery of America," wrote Dostoevsky, "for Asia still remains undiscovered for us. Our penetration into Asia will uplift our spirit and strengthen us. As soon as we recover our independence we shall see our task in regard to Europe more clearly; during the last two centuries we have lost the habit of work and have become lazy talkers." He ends his article by prophesying that the unexplored and neglected vastness of Siberia contains an inexhaustible wealth of coal and minerals, and that their exploitation, together with the development of agriculture there, will make Russia prosperous and at the same time open the door to the spiritual influence of her Christian culture for Oriental people.

His last call, imploring the Russians to stop being ashamed of their Asiatic connections, was one of the impressive instances of historic foresight. The policy advocated by Dostoevsky was applied in practice at last in the twentieth century, and its beneficial fruits have been exactly those predicted by him.

Such are some of Dostoevsky's thoughts about Russia, Europe and the future of Christian civilisation. He was a perplexing writer, and his life and works contain many contradictions which have not yet been solved and probably will never be solved. He had exceptional insight into the future, he knew men as probably nobody else knew them, and he was familiar with evil in all its most destructive forms.

He met Christ, however, in one of his darkest hours, and was saved by Him from despair and mental and physical disintegration. He was never free of suffering; he had to struggle hard to the very end, and yet he accepted and valued life and praised his Creator. It was given to him to see in all its terrifying reality the great battle between good and evil, and he was sorrowfully aware that mankind was approaching its most decisive stage. It is no wonder that he bitterly attacked those false prophets of liberalism and emancipation who promised an earthly paradise to their naïve followers, and that he had no patience with the quack doctors who wanted to save mankind from suffering without attempting to cure it of sin and death.

All his life Dostoevsky wrote under pressure. He never had time to elaborate or explain his daring visions and prophetic intuitions; this difficult task was undertaken by his young friend and disciple, Vladimir Sergeevich Soloviev.

Chapter Four

SOLOVIEV

VLADIMIR SOLOVIEV was born on January 16th, 1853, in Moscow. His father, Sergei Mikhailovich, a well-known professor of Moscow University and author of a monumental history of Russia, was a typical scholar, a man absorbed in his books and manuscripts, who kept himself aloof even from his family, and evoked from his children respect rather than warm affection. Under an appearance of scholarly detachment, Sergei Soloviev preserved a genuine devotion to religion. He was a staunch churchman, attended church services regularly, and brought up his children in the same tradition. He belonged to an old clerical family, and Vladimir Soloviev inherited from his father love for the Church, missionary zeal, realism and a bent for study.

On his mother's side Soloviev had quite a different background. She came from the south of Russia, and had both Polish and Ukrainian blood in her veins. She was an emotional and warm-hearted, yet shy and self-effacing woman, who devoted her life to her husband and children. She too was deeply religious and highly imaginative, and from her Soloviev inherited his sense of humour, his love for poetry and his mystical tendency, the character of which suggested rather the Western than the Eastern tradition.

These two strains of his inheritance never wholly amalgamated in Soloviev's personality; they remained distinct, sometimes even conflicting. He was at once a scholar and a mystic, a philosopher and a poet, a critic and an enthusiast. He could never fit into any ordinary frame of life. He was always on the move, ready to abandon everything in obedience to some sudden call to new adventure. He spent his whole life in public, was very popular and had many friends; and yet he was an exceptionally lonely and enigmatic figure. He had many relatives, but no family; he was more than once in love, but never married; he was a keen promoter of Christian unity, yet none of the Churches could claim his complete allegiance. He was a leader of many movements and yet could not be identified with any one of them.

SOLOVIEV

Soloviev died on the threshold of the twentieth century and he foresaw the main trend of the new epoch. His mind was preoccupied with problems which were to reveal their full significance only years after his death. He was the first man in Russia to give warning of the growing menace of Japan, he was the forerunner among the Orthodox of the Œcumenical movement, he prepared the ground for the renewal of the social action of the Church, and was promoter of religious co-operation between the Jews and the Christians. He inaugurated a new period in the history of Russian philosophy, theology and poetry, and his contributions to all of them were of lasting value. There is hardly any problem of the present troubled period which he did not foresee or which failed to find a response in his sensitive mind. He was a man of unusual insight, so much ahead of the average man of his generation in his foreknowledge of the events to come that to his contemporaries he appeared to be eccentric.

Soloviev was a philosopher equally balanced between scholarship and speculation; his most challenging ideas are presented with elegance, urbanity and learning. He was reticent about his inner life, yet his philosophical thought, his social and political theories, were all the fruit of his rare mystical intuitions. Only towards the end of his life did Soloviev resolve to communicate his greatest spiritual experience. But even then he was reluctant to reveal himself fully, and chose the form of a poem which leaves its readers in doubt whether the author is in earnest or merely making fun of himself and his audience.

This poem, "Three Meetings," is of cardinal importance for the study of Soloviev's personality, for, in spite of its irony and intentional triviality of tone, it is the most significant autobiographical fragment among his writings. In this poem Soloviev stated that three times in his life he had had a revelation of the glory and unity of the created world. This knowledge was given to him in visions of Sophia, the Divine Wisdom—who appeared to him as a woman of unsurpassable beauty. He saw her first in Moscow on Ascension Day during the celebration of the Holy Eucharist when he was a boy of nine; the second time in the Reading Room of the British Museum, whilst he was working there on his post-graduate thesis; and again the same year in the desert in Egypt, whither an inner voice had called him to await the vision. For Soloviev, these three meetings were neither the illusions of a distorted mind nor poetical objectifications of emotional state; they were cardinal facts, on which he built up his entire outlook. His philosophical works were an attempt to systematise the meaning of these meetings; his religious and social activities were the outcome of his desire to relate them to the daily course of his life. Neither his thought nor his personality can be understood without constant reference to this well-spring of his creative inspiration. Soloviev himself never doubted the reality of his encounters with the Divine Wisdom, a privilege which he found some other mystics claimed to have shared.[1]

The meeting with Sophia at the age of nine is evidence enough that Soloviev was an unusual child. He was endowed with vivid imagination, and lived in a world of his own, where all his possessions were living persons, having their proper names, and maintaining lively relations with their young owner.

At the age of fourteen he passed through his first religious crisis. He lost his faith in God; but he could not remain indifferent. Soloviev by nature was a missionary, and when he became an atheist he tried to destroy faith in others with the same zeal with which he sought to regain people to Christianity in the later periods of his life. His militant atheism led him to acts of sacrilege. One evening, in the presence of his astounded school friends, young Soloviev destroyed his ikons, in front of which as a child he had offered so many ardent prayers. Young Soloviev passionately denied the reality of that spiritual world of which the ikons are visible signs, and his act of destruction was intended to demonstrate to his friends that he was right.

All his religious fervour in the years of his adolescence was given to the belief in the illimitable possibilities of natural science. He preached that philosophical materialism could solve all the problems of human life and was the only guarantee of human happiness and progress. In accordance with these convictions, he entered the Faculty of Science at the age of seventeen.

The Russian universities of that period were filled with young men who believed in Darwinism as a new religion, and treated atheism as the last word in human wisdom. Intolerant of any other point of view, entirely dogmatic and uncritical as far as their own creed was concerned, they regarded all who dared to doubt the truth of materialism as morally suspect. Soloviev was too intelligent to be satisfied for long with this naïve faith in progress and evolution. He began to shift away from the position occupied by the majority of students, and in 1872 he broke away

[1] Jacob Boehme, Swedenborg, Paracelsus, George Gishtel, Gottfried Arnold, John Pordage.

from the creed which he had so ardently preached for six years. He left the Faculty of Science, began the study of philosophy, and in 1873 graduated in Arts, with the best degree of his year.

Soloviev was never the man for compromise or vacillation. From militant atheism he went straight back to the full profession of religion. His studies of philosophy were accompanied by the reading of the Fathers. In the course of the academic year 1873-4, he committed an act which caused great scandal. It was the first indication that Soloviev was not afraid to challenge social conventions and defy public opinion. This revolutionary step was his decision to attend lectures at the Theological Academy of the Monastery of St. Sergius, near Moscow. In most countries there would be nothing unusual in a young man interested in philosophy and religion becoming a theological student, but in the Russia of the nineteenth century it was a portent. The gulf between the Westernised classes of Russian society and the clergy, supposedly mere puppets of the bureaucracy, was so deep that the students of theology lived in a world apart, a kind of intellectual ghetto. No representative of the intelligentsia could imagine that any useful purpose could be served by attending lectures at a theological academy; no professors or students of theology could believe that anybody not bred in a seminary could enter their schools except as a spy.

Soloviev was regarded by his former friends as an apostate; his action seemed to them to be a deliberate self-degradation. By his new colleagues he was received with mixed feelings of curiosity and suspicion. Soloviev himself profited by his studies. He found the intellectual standard of professors and students higher in the Academy than in the University, and the general atmosphere less charged with narrow sectarianism and intolerant dogmatism than in the Faculty of Science. Professor M. D. Muretov, who was Soloviev's contemporary, has left the following description of him at this period: "A small, rather round face, pale, almost bluish; big, very dark eyes without life or expression, permanently gazing into the far distance, black eyebrows, sharply marked, long, thin hands with pale, nerveless fingers, long legs encased in tight, threadbare trousers; a long, thin, dark, self-centred and enigmatic creature."

Such was the impression Soloviev produced upon his fellow students. But he paid little attention to them, spending most of his time over his books; he was absorbed in the study of Western philosophy, the Eastern Fathers, mystics and occultists. He was preoccupied with an ambitious plan of writing an irrefutable repudiation of philosophical positivism and materialism which should deliver a crushing blow to the popular creed professed by the youth of his generation.

This was his aim in the thesis he presented in 1874, *The Crisis of Western Philosophy*. It was an able work, much influenced by the writings of the Slavophils, especially Ivan Kireevski (1806–56). Its main contention was that the individualism and rationalism of European culture had sapped its creative strength; and that the synthesis between faith and reason, without which no further progress was possible, would be achieved, not by Europe, but by the Christian East.

The thesis caused the sensation that might have been expected. The boldness of Soloviev's attack on positivism, his odd personal appearance, his claim to foretell the future course of thought, provoked the admiration of some and the bitter hostility of others. The radical Press described him as a dangerous reactionary, while his more philosophical opponents denounced him as a blind obscurantist. Yet Soloviev's thesis showed such penetration, originality and freshness of approach that, in spite of criticisms, he was offered a lectureship at Moscow University and he was also invited to teach philosophy at the newly founded Women's University College.

The road to a professorial chair lay open; Soloviev's academic career seemed assured, but he was not made to follow in his father's footsteps. He lectured for a year, and then applied for a travelling scholarship, and went to London to study Eastern religions and mysticism.

Eighteen hundred and seventy-five witnessed another crisis in his life. He was twenty-three. He had regained his faith in the truth of Christianity and was intellectually equipped for the task of its philosophical defence, but he was still only at the beginning of his long search for the full meaning of the Church. He was equally interested in historic Christendom and in some esoteric sects. At this period of his life he was, for instance, much attracted by spiritualism, and one of the reasons for his choice of London was the fact that it was the centre of that movement. Soloviev was still uncertain of his direction till it was determined for him by his second meeting with Sophia.

On his arrival in England he plunged into the study of the theory and practice of mysticism. He read widely, and attended the meetings of spiritualists and other occultists, without finding what he sought. He lived in a state of expectancy, and believed that some important revelation would shortly be given to him.

Ordinary life hardly existed for him in those days; London, its people, sights, churches and museums, all seemed unreal and shadowy. He never saw England with his eyes open and it left no impression on him.[1]

Soloviev's expectations were justified. In the Reading Room of the British Museum occurred the decisive event which altered the whole course of his life. His academic career was ended before it had begun, his relations with other people, especially women, were changed, his philosophical and religious activities took a new and unexpected turn.

Soloviev described this turning-point in his life in the poem, "Three Meetings." He saw in the dim light of an autumn day in London, amidst books and manuscripts, the same Sophia who had appeared to him in Moscow in the far-off days of his childhood. He was at once grieved and elated, for he could not make out the whole figure of his beloved. He was enchanted, however, when he heard a voice ordering him to go to Egypt, and without hesitation he obeyed the call. On October 14th he sent a short, intentionally casual, note to his mother informing her that his studies required his immediate departure for the East. Two days later he left London, and, at the end of November, his ardent longing for another meeting was satisfied. He was granted his crowning revelation of the Divine Wisdom. This was the third of his three meetings.

He met her this time alone in the desert at dawn, when the transfigured and reintegrated Universe appeared before him in its original splendour and glory.

This expedition almost cost young Soloviev his life. When he was wandering alone in the desert, dressed all in black, he was attacked by Bedouins, who took him for the Devil, but realised their mistake in time and let him go unharmed.

Mystical experience is essentially private and incommunicable. The mystic may say that he has been in bliss. He may try to hint at the nature of this bliss by using images of gentle heat or blinding light. Those who have had some inkling of similar experiences

[1] It is noteworthy that a Slavophil like Khomiakov was intensely interested in every detail of European life and delighted in many English customs and traditions, whilst Soloviev, who called himself a "Westerniser," was bored by Europe, and visited foreign countries only to find the verification of his own hypotheses.

may recognise them in what he says. But to those whose pre-conceptions drive them to deny the existence of any supernatural being, it is all waste of breath or ink. The man felt warm, or dazed, and that is that. Soloviev was aware that his efforts to describe his meeting with Sophia would be ridiculed by many, and he armed himself against these impending attacks by making fun of him-self—the unworthy recipient of the heavenly revelation. But his object in going to Egypt was achieved; there he saw the Divine Wisdom in all her beauty and glory. There was nothing else to tempt him to linger in Egypt, or, for the matter of that, in Europe. So in Cairo he remained till the expiry of the leave of absence granted with his scholarship.

The well-known French writer, M. de Vogüé,[1] who met Soloviev in Cairo, gives a description of him at this period: "To have seen his face once, was to remember him for ever; pale, thin, framed in his long, slightly curling hair, his face with its beautiful regular features was entirely dominated by his great eyes, wonderful, penetrating, visionary eyes. Such faces must have inspired the monastic painters of the past who sought a model for the Christ of their ikons. It was the face of Christ as seen by the Slav people—the loving, meditative, sorrowful Christ." De Vogüé adds: "Young Soloviev, in spite of the hot weather, wore the long black cloak and silk hat with which he had left London."

In the autumn of 1876 Soloviev returned to Moscow. He came back a changed man, and his academic career, so happily begun, no longer held any attraction for him. The opposition to his teaching was stiffer, and in February, 1877, Soloviev resigned his lectureship and moved to St. Petersburg, where he obtained a minor post in the Department of Education.

For the next few years he gave his main attention to the formu-lation of his philosophical position, and at the same time took an increasingly active part in the social and religious movements of the country. His personal life was enriched by the friendship of two outstanding women, Countess Sophia Andreevna Tolstaia, the widow of the famous poet, Alexei Tolstoy, and her niece, Sophia Petrovna Hitrovo. He was also much influenced by Dostoevsky, with whom he was closely associated in these years. In 1877 Soloviev published *The Philosophic Foundation of Integral Knowledge*;

1 *Sous l'horizon. Hommes et choses d'hier*, Paris, 1905.

in 1878 a *Treatise on Godmanhood*. In 1877–80 appeared his monumental work, *The Criticism of Abstract Principles*.

For him this was a time of fruitful intellectual work, and growing popularity. Soloviev still shared in the main the Slavophil outlook, and in his public speeches he echoed many of Dostoevsky's favourite ideas. He believed in Russia's special mission to find the synthesis between the East, with its pantheism, and the West, with its emancipated man who had lost the sense of the Divine. Soloviev exalted the qualities of the common Russian people with their profound sense of humility and readiness to forgive, and he called the Russian intelligentsia to repent, to give up their aping of the West, and to return to the outlook of the Orthodox peasants. But if Soloviev was impressed with Dostoevsky, the latter too acknowledged the influence of his brilliant young friend. He was at once attracted and disturbed by the unusual combination in Soloviev of logical thought with mystical intuition. It is supposed that the character of Ivan Karamazov, the believing sceptic, is Dostoevsky's portrait of Soloviev. Soloviev's position was unique; he was the only man who could fill the largest halls in St. Petersburg or Moscow, lecturing on philosophy or Christian belief. In spite of the positivism and irreligion of the Russian educated classes, in spite of the popularity of Nihilism among the university students, he could stir the minds and hearts of his crowded audiences, and even managed to bring back a number of his listeners to the Christian faith. No philosopher could compete with him for a hearing in Russia. His works were crowned with a doctorate, but still no university offered him a chair.

His success did not last long after its climax in 1881. In the winter of 1880–1 he had delivered a course of public lectures in St. Petersburg which was attended by crowds of eager listeners, chiefly students. On March 1st, 1881, the Emperor Alexander II (1856–81), the liberator of the serfs, was assassinated by a group of extremists who believed that the death of the Tsar would start a general uprising. Their expectations were not fulfilled; on the contrary, this act of barbarism roused general indignation, and deprived the revolutionary movement of the sympathy and support even of those who desired to see political changes in Russia.

Soloviev was no revolutionary. Every form of cruelty and destruction was abhorrent to his mind, and in his lectures he attacked those who entertained the hope of bringing happiness and progress to the Russian people by means of violence and deceit. On March 28th he delivered his concluding lecture. His last words staggered everybody. They were directly addressed to the new Emperor, Alexander III (1881–94). Soloviev made a vigorous appeal to him to forgive the murderers of his father, and thus to show the whole world that Russia was indeed a Christian country.[1] The manuscript of his speech has not been preserved; accounts of his words vary: but all agree that the effect produced by them was terrific. After a moment of tense silence the crowd rose to its feet. There were shouts of "Traitor!" and "Murderer!" and equally vehement cries of approval. Next day Soloviev sent a letter to the Emperor explaining his position. He wrote: "The present sorrowful time gives to the Russian Tsar an unparalleled opportunity to reveal the power of Christian forgiveness, and to achieve a great moral victory which will raise his authority to a height never attained before, and establish his realm on an unshakable foundation. By showing mercy to the enemies of his throne, against all the dictates and calculations of worldly wisdom, the Tsar will rise to a more than human height, and by this act will demonstrate the divine ground of his authority and show that in him resides the supreme spiritual power of the whole Russian people."[2]

Soloviev's uninvited interference met with strong disapproval in Court circles. The new Emperor was indignant. Some of Soloviev's friends even feared his banishment to Siberia, but the only penalty he suffered was an order restraining him from lecturing in public for an indefinite period. It is doubtful, whether Soloviev really expected the act of forgiveness that he called for. It looked rather as if his appeal had been made in a spirit of self-sacrifice for that cause in which he ardently believed, and which both he and Dostoevsky wanted to see triumphant in Russia—the cause of a free Christian theocracy.

The speech of March, 1881, marked the end of Soloviev's association with the Slavophils, as well as the end of his public lectures, and the final blow to his hope of a professorial chair. Soloviev saw that Russia in her isolation was not able to realise the theocratic order of his dreams and turned his attention to the West, where he expected to find the shortcomings in his own Church and nation supplied. In his short autobiography, written in 1887,

---

[1] An aversion against capital punishment has always been strong in Russia. The Empress Elizabeth (1741–61) abolished it altogether. Alexander II, again, greatly restrained its application. During forty-eight years from 1855 till 1903 in the Empire inhabited by 170,000,000, only 114 men were condemned to death.

[2] E. Radlov, *V. Soloviev's Letters*, Vol. IV, St. Petersburg, 1923.

he defined the object of his work after 1881 as the reunion of the
Church and the reconciliation of Christianity and Judaism.

The next ten years of Soloviev's life (1881–91) were his most
creative period. Inspired by his strong faith in the righteousness
of his cause, he dedicated all his energy to the breaking down of
the age-old barriers dividing the Western and Eastern Churches,
and the creation of a better understanding between the Christian
and the Jew. It was a period of many new contacts and friendships, of several journeys abroad, of high hopes and bitter
disappointments.

When Soloviev began his work for Church unity he was still
closely associated with the Slavophils, but Dostoevsky's death in
1881 and Soloviev's increasing attraction to the universalism of
the Roman Church alienated him from his former supporters,
and brought him over to the camp of their adversaries, the
Westernisers. The latter, however, were either indifferent or hostile
to Soloviev's confidence in the power of the Church, and his
association with them was marred by suspicion and misunderstanding.

Soloviev was equally misunderstood by his new Roman Catholic
friends, who at first enthusiastically welcomed him, thinking to
find in him a convert of the usual type. But they were soon disillusioned, for Soloviev had his own ideas about the Roman Church
and was critical of many of its features.

His contacts with the Roman Catholics began in 1884. Soloviev
was then absorbed in the writing of his great work, *The History
and Future of Theocracy*. It contained an ardent plea for the
restoration of unity between the Latin and the Orthodox Churches.
A visitor to Moscow, the Croat Canon Frančisc Rački, brought
Soloviev in touch with the famous Croat Bishop of Diakovo,
Mgr. Strossmayer. These two outstanding clerics were enthusiastic
supporters of the Slavonic cause, and they welcomed Soloviev as
representative of a new movement which should re-establish the
unity of all Slav peoples, though not (as the Slavophils had advocated) in the fold of the Orthodox Church, but under the auspices
of the Roman See. Mgr. Strossmayer, however, was firmly
opposed to the Latinisation of the Slavonic Christians, and to the
excessive claims of the Roman Curia. He was one of the few
prelates who protested against the promulgation of papal infallibility at the Vatican Council of 1870, and he hoped that Rome
would be prepared to grant a wider autonomy to the Slavonic
Churches if they all accepted her primacy. Soloviev, with his

I

grandiose theocratic plans, with his belief that Russia was called to play a leading part in the destiny of mankind, but that nothing could be achieved till the schism between East and West was healed, was greeted with delight and admiration by the learned and saintly Bishop. Strossmayer and Soloviev were mutually attracted to each other. Their outlook, their hopes, their plans were alike; they both were idealists, little practised in the intricacies of ecclesiastical diplomacy. Soloviev's visit to Diakovo in 1886 was one of the happiest events of his life. He wrote to his brother that the eighteen days he spent with the Bishop were one delightful festival. As the outcome of this meeting, Soloviev drew up a manifesto on the reunion of the Churches. He expressed in it his willingness to accept the Roman Primacy, but insisted that the Eastern Church must retain after reunion its complete autonomy. He particularly emphasised the important position of the Russian Tsar as a successor of the Byzantine Emperors, and ascribed to him a special divinely appointed function in the life of the universal Church.

The years 1886–8 form the culminating point of Soloviev's attraction to Rome; he remained formally a member of the Russian Church, but he tried to identify his outlook as closely as possible with Latin Catholicism. Bishop Strossmayer shared the hopes of his Russian friend. He personally took Soloviev's statement to Rome, and it is possible that he arranged for Soloviev a private audience with the Pope in 1888, but so far no document has been published confirming this fact.

The bright expectations entertained by the two Slavs were not shared by the better-informed and experienced French Jesuits, who also took a keen interest in Soloviev and his schemes. They wanted to meet him personally, and in the spring of 1888 Soloviev again went abroad. This time the object of his journey was not the small and friendly town of Diakovo, but Paris. He carried with him the manuscript of a new work, in French, entitled *Russia and the Universal Church*, to which he attached great importance. Soloviev's feelings towards the Russian Church at the moment were embittered by the policy of the newly appointed Procurator of the Synod, Konstantin Pobedonostsev. The Procurator was an able man, but deeply mistrustful of human nature and therefore opposed to all progressive and liberal movements. He possessed a powerful personality, and till his death in 1905 he was the principal promoter of reaction, in both the political and the ecclesiastical life of the country.

He and Soloviev stood in irreconcilable opposition to each other; for Pobedonostsev every step towards freedom was a step nearer disaster, whilst Soloviev ardently believed in the coming victory of Christianity, and the possibility of the establishment of a free theocratic order here on earth. Pobedonostsev treated Soloviev's Utopianism as highly subversive, for though, like Pobedonostsev himself, Soloviev was both a Christian and a monarchist, he sought to make both Church and Empire the leaders in the progressive movements of his time, and this was to the powerful Procurator a dangerous perversion of most sacred ideals.

It was when Pobedonostsev stopped the publication of Soloviev's book on theocracy that the latter realised to the full the humiliating helplessness of the Russian Church. Soloviev came to Paris less as an advocate of Church unity than as an indignant accuser of his own supine fellow Churchmen and countrymen. On his arrival in France, he published a pamphlet, *L'Idée Russe*,[1] and an article, *Saint Vladimir et l'Etat Chrétien*,[2] in which he sharply criticised the position of the Church in Russia. In contention that the life of the Eastern Church was paralysed by that submission to the State which, first evident in the Byzantine Empire, in Russia had been renewed and perpetuated, he went so far as to declare that the Old Believers, not the Orthodox, represented the true Church in Russia.

Such extravagances, bred of exasperation, by no means indicated that Soloviev had ceased to care for reunion. In his book *La Russie et l'Eglise Universelle*,[3] he now advocated reunion by means of an alliance between the Pope and the Russian Emperor. He still continued to ascribe to Russia a leading part in the establishment of a theocratic order, but he looked to the consecrated monarch rather than to the Church which gave him his hallowing to end her self-imposed isolation. The united efforts of the Roman Pontiff, representing the Fatherhood of God, and of the Russian Emperor his obedient son, assisted by a renewed ministry of prophets, organs of the Holy Spirit, would be able, according to Soloviev, to reveal the full regenerating power of the Church and secure the complete victory of Christianity. In the third and last part of his book, Soloviev expanded his ideas on the cosmic implications of Trinitarian doctrine, and ended with the definition of the part played in the life of the cosmos by Sophia, the Divine revelation of the unity, harmony and beauty of the created world.

[1] Ed. Didier-Perrin, Paris, 1888. [2] *L'Univers*, No. 4, 11, 19, 1888.
[3] Ed. Albert Savine, Paris, 1889.

The six months Soloviev spent in Paris was a trying period. He was received by French Roman Catholics with a courtesy not wholly free from condescension. He was invited to speak in fashionable drawing-rooms, where clerics, society ladies and distinguished members of the Academy were good enough to listen to the ardent orations of a Russian philosopher. At the end of his speeches he was congratulated with equal sincerity on his command of French and on his laudable desire to submit to the Holy See. The interest of his audiences was confined to the possibility of his conversion, and they welcomed Soloviev as the first-fruit of the coming harvest of Russia, while Soloviev's most cherished ideas on theocracy, the Trinitarian structure of the Church and the Sophian principle of the beauty and harmony of the cosmos were deplored by his new friends as whimsical weaknesses. The French Jesuits were frankly alarmed by the Slav mysticism of this prospective convert. They insisted that the last part of his book, the theological section, should be omitted as unsuitable for publication, and advised him to show an example of obedience by submitting to Rome, like other converts, unconditionally. Soloviev refused. He was no ordinary convert; his interest in Rome was only a part of his lifelong devotion to Sophia, which had led him from one sacrifice to another, and accounted for the abrupt changes and apparent inconsistencies of his conduct. His book was published as it stood. But hardly anyone in France could follow its argument. It produced no effect, and Soloviev realised that he had failed completely. In later Polish Catholic editions of the book the author's conclusion was finally suppressed; but even thus mutilated, the work made little appeal to the Roman world.[1]

The Christmas of 1888 Soloviev spent with his faithful friend, Bishop Strossmayer, in Diakovo. They were both delighted to meet again. Their affection was unimpaired, but they themselves had changed. Both felt in the depth of their hearts that their plans for reunion were beyond realisation. Strossmayer recounted to Soloviev the Pope's comment on his pamphlet, *L'Idée Russe*: "*Bella idea, ma, fuor d'un miracolo, e cosa impossibile.*' The Head of the Roman Church had put the final seal of rejection on Soloviev's project. Only a miracle could bring about the unity of the Church,

[1] Mgr. d'Herbigny, a Roman Catholic admirer of Soloviev, makes, for instance, the following comment: "We have already referred to the somewhat strange character of the third part. Its very title, 'The Trinitarian Principle and its Social Application,' might well cause surprise" (*V. Soloviev, a Russian Newman*, London, 1918, p. 220).

but, except for a few eccentrics like Soloviev and Strossmayer, no one asked for the miracle to happen, and therefore there was little chance that it would. The reconciliation between the Roman and the Eastern Churches had to wait till the time when the desire for unity should become operative in the hearts and minds of many of their members. Soloviev's hopes of seeing the Roman Pontiff and the Orthodox Emperor embrace had proved to be as premature as his call to the Tsar to pardon the murderers of his father.

While Soloviev was still absorbed in his work for Christian reunion, he was already giving much of his time and attention to the study of Judaism. Between 1881 and 1891 Soloviev published several articles on the Jewish question. He made friends among Russian Jews, and learned Hebrew. In an important article (published in 1884), "Judaism and the Christian Question," Soloviev stated that the Jewish problem was fundamental for the Christian Church, and that anti-Semitism and indifference to the religious destiny of the Jews were equally contrary to the spirit of Christianity. He remained till his end a faithful friend of the Jews, and his public protests against oppressive measures directed against them by the Government won him many friends and admirers among Russian Jewry.

To the same active decade of Soloviev's life belongs his friendship with several outstanding thinkers and writers: Nikolai Feodorov (1828–1903), the most paradoxical of Russian thinkers; the brilliant and ironical Konstantin Leontiev (1831–91), the Russian Nietzsche; and the elegant lyrical poet, Afanasi Fet (1820–92). He was closely associated also with Lev Tolstoy (1828–1910), with whom he shared certain convictions, such as his opposition to capital punishment, but from whom he differed strongly on other and equally important points. Soloviev's Romanising tendency had by now brought him into sharp opposition to his former friends, like Ivan Aksakov (1823–86).

Soloviev even attacked the Slavophils in print. He sharply criticised Strakhov (1828–96), Katkov (1820–87) and Danilevski (1822–85), the representatives of Russian national exclusiveness; and, identifying them with the old founders of the Slavophil movement, condemned both together as narrow-minded Chauvinists, forgetting the debt he owed to such men as Ivan Kireevski and Alexei Khomiakov.

To the same period belongs another of his remarkable books, *The Spiritual Foundations of Life* (1882–4). This outlines a consistent Christian philosophy of life covering both personal problems and the task of Christian social action. It contained new ideas borrowed from the teaching of Feodorov, who, in his work, *The Common Cause*, called Christians to unite in an effort to defeat their greatest enemies, disunity, disease and death.

This period of great creative effort ended without bringing Soloviev any appreciable success. Nowhere could he see the approach of victory for his views. On all sides he met with indifference, suspicion or open hostility. The last nine years of his life (1891–1900) were full of doubts and intense inner struggle, but they were also the time of the final maturing of his personality and of liberation from those elements of occultism and eroticism which had so far marred his Christian view of life. The collapse of his reunion schemes provoked in Soloviev a reaction against organised Christianity; he lost faith in Roman Catholicism and Eastern Orthodoxy alike; he felt that the years given to his attempts to bring them together had been wasted; that both papacy and Russian autocracy were unable and unwilling to act. His reaction from the enthusiasms of the previous decade was aggravated by more personal causes. He fell in love with a woman who had little in common with him. Only after a long struggle and humiliation did he gain the strength to break away from her. Soloviev had many romantic friendships, some short, some lasting. All had deep influence on him. Soloviev was a seeker who could find no satisfaction either in the many causes he championed or the many women he loved. He could not be constant: but he was never shallow nor, at bottom, inconsistent. His last love caused him great pain, but it helped to produce one of the most original of his philosophical essays, *The Meaning of Love*. The depth and freshness of this work had been purchased at the cost of a life of tempestuous passion and generous devotion, never crowned with peace. Soloviev believed that he had found the secret of the strange affinity between erotic love, with its heat and passion, and the serenity and joy of the great mystical revelations.

In these years of new ventures in the search for truth, Soloviev again returned to philosophy. His monumental work, *The Justification of the Good* (1897), belongs to this period. It is written with vigour and a deep sense of conviction. He was still only forty-five, but he felt that his life was nearly ended. He had never spared himself, never cared for his own comfort; he gave all he had to the causes which he served, and in these few crowded years he did more than most men could do in twice the time. Soloviev knew that his work was over, and he revisited the places which were sacred for him. In 1898 he went for the second time to Egypt and saw again the place where he met Sophia. On his return, he wrote the poem, "Three Meetings," in which he revealed that greatest experience of his life.

Soloviev, in these last years, was a striking figure. He was known all over Russia. His philosophy was not shared by many, but he was esteemed for his sincerity and his many achievements. He was always surrounded by people—not only those who came to hear some word of wisdom from this great Russian teacher, but for the most part people who wanted advice or alms. He was incapable of laying out his time in the normal way. He had no home of his own, and stayed either in hotels or with friends. As soon as he stopped anywhere, a crowd of admirers, friends and petitioners besieged him; some of them wanted to consult him on spiritual matters, others wanted to read him their manuscripts, others asked for letters of introduction to men of influence and power. Still others simply begged for money, and none was ever refused help. Soloviev knew well that many of his visitors were only failures and frauds, but he thought that these were in even greater need than others, and he was ready to go without food himself rather than let them leave empty-handed. When he had no money left, he borrowed from his friends to give to rogues and drunkards. He himself led an ascetic life; he never ate meat, seldom slept in a bed, constantly forgot his meals, and worked all night because his day was taken up by others. Once, during the whole Russian winter, he went without a warm overcoat, having given away his own to a poor student and being without money to buy another. His friends vigorously protested against such conduct and tried to interfere, but gave up their efforts as hopeless. Though he was at the disposal of all, he remained solitary. His life was dedicated to a sacred cause, and everyone who came in contact with him realised the presence of an unknown power in the childlike and helpless philosopher who looked twice his age. Only children and animals felt quite at home with him.

An important event marked the approach of the end of his earthly struggle. On February 18th, 1896, he received the Sacrament, for the first and last time, from a Uniat priest, Fr. Nicholas Tolstoy, in Moscow. This act has often been interpreted in the Roman Catholic Press as Soloviev's conversion to Rome. This is a misleading statement. When, ten years earlier, he was full of enthusiasm for the papacy, he made no attempt to communicate at Latin altars. In 1896 he no longer believed in the immediate reunion of the Churches; moreover, he had lost his faith in the importance of ecclesiastical organisations. He longed for the coming of Œcumenical Christianity, and felt that the historic Churches had to disappear and to give place to some new and higher realisation of Christian truth. His communion at the Roman altar was a prophetic act demonstrating his belief that no barriers built by men could break the unity within the Church of Christ. Soloviev had no intention of abandoning his membership of the Orthodox Church, and in 1897, a year after his supposed conversion to Rome, being ill, he asked his friend, the Rev. Professor A. Ivantsov-Platonov, to hear his confession and to give him Communion. Ivantsov-Platonov heard the confession, but refused to communicate Soloviev, for the latter was unwilling to recognise that by communicating at the Roman altar he had acted in disregard of ecclesiastical discipline. On his death-bed Soloviev changed his mind; after a long confession, he received Holy Communion from the Orthodox priest, Fr. Beliaev, and died reconciled with the Church of his fathers, which he criticised so sharply during his stormy life. In the last year he wrote his prophetic work, *Three Conversations on War, Progress, and the End of History*. In this book he repudiated many of his hitherto cherished ideals. It was given to him before the end to see still greater truths than he had been able to understand in the years of his intense intellectual activity. He himself considered this last work to be the most important of all that he had written. The whole book is dominated by an acute feeling of the existence of a personal evil. This was a radical departure from the position held by Soloviev throughout his life. He had been an optimist who believed in social progress and Church reunion and minimised the importance of sin and evil. As a young man, though already converted to Christianity, Soloviev used to say that he believed in God, but could not believe in the existence of the Devil. In his last book he showed clearly that he was obliged to revise his convictions. There is evidence from Soloviev's conversations with his closest friends, and from some of his poems, that something very unexpected and terrifying happened to him on a boat in 1898, when he went for the second time to Egypt. It is difficult not to feel behind his story of the anti-Christ that he had suffered some unusual experience of meeting with the evil one. Soloviev was convinced that his approaching death was connected with the events of 1898.

He died at the age of forty-seven; he fell ill on July 14th, 1900; with great effort he reached the country house of his friend and former pupil, the philosopher Prince Sergei Trubetskoy (*d.* 1907). The doctors could do nothing for him. Soloviev's whole organism seemed exhausted. On July 17th he made his confession and received Holy Communion. After that his strength ebbed rapidly. He was not afraid of death, and he knew that his end was coming. He prayed much aloud, especially for the Jewish people. He recited in Hebrew psalms which he knew by heart. He died in the evening on July 31st, without pain, and in complete peace of mind. His last words were: "Work, for the Lord is hard." His funeral service was held in the Chapel of Moscow University, where, as a boy of nine years old, he saw his first vision of the Divine Wisdom.

The basic intuition of Soloviev's life was his vision of creation as an all-embracing unity (*vse-edinstvo*). The cosmos was for him an organism, animated by one spirit, moving towards a definite goal. "The whole visible world is no haphazard collection of 'made' things; it is the continuous development and growth of a living organism" (VII, 12).[1]

Soloviev had the rare gift of seeing the swiftly changing scenery of life as a single process. His theology and philosophy, his plans for social reform, his schemes for Church reunion, his attitude to Russia and Europe, his theories on science and on sex were all the outcome of his fundamental conviction that the universe was designed according to a plan, and that the mind of the Architect was discernible behind the distracting variety of phenomenal existence.

The Creator loves His creation, and because love has meaning only if it is mutual, God endowed the cosmos with the gift of freedom and made it capable of entering into personal relation with Him. "God is love: the fullness of Divine Love demands complete and mutual unity with *the Other*. But such unity presupposes the self-existing and self-actuating attitude of this other to the Creator" (IV, 337).

Soloviev was convinced that belief in a Personal God implies that the cosmos also has a personality; to this personality he gave the name of Hagia Sophia, or the Divine Wisdom who responded by a free act of her own love to the creative love of her Maker.

[1] This and further quotations are made from Soloviev's works published in 1911 in Moscow; they refer to the volume and page of that edition.

This personal relation between the Creator and the creature, however, reached its full expression only when man appeared on the earthly scene. Cosmic life, passive and unconscious at first, through a long process of evolution in the vegetable and animal kingdom, was raised in man to the level of understanding of its ultimate purpose, and of responsible participation in its fulfilment. "Perfect possession rests on free consent and the active response of the possessed. Such perfect dominion, or, in other words, true theocracy (which is the same thing as the realisation of Divine love), requires a creature capable of entering into a reciprocal relation with God, for the sake of complete union with Him" (IV, 337).

By the word "theocracy" Soloviev meant co-operation between the Creator and the creature, and he described the conditions its achievement requires. Theocracy needed that the creatures should possess "freedom to choose the right side, reason capable of searching for truth, and that whole-hearted desire for perfection which makes possible active participation in the divine ordinance of the cosmos" (IV, 338). Among all earthly beings only man satisfied all these conditions.

The cosmos was for Soloviev a person; he was intensely aware of the unity of its life, but at the same time he was opposed to every form of pantheism, for the ultimate goal of evolution was not the absorption of everything in an impersonal Deity, but, on the contrary, the establishment of personal relation between God and man, the spokesman and the morally responsible representative of creation. This attitude implied that unique value belonged to each individual.

"Each human being can become a living reflection of the Absolute, a conscious and independent organ of the cosmic life" (VII, 14). But in order to apprehend the truth, to grasp the purpose of life, man must first overcome his own grievous limitations, must end his inner ˙scord, the chief expression of which is his self-centredness and egoism. The isolation of an individual from the rest of the cosmos blinds him to the greater reality of life, and leads him into a realm of illusion. "The root of imperfect existence lies in the exclusion by one creature of all others. True life consists of living in another as in oneself" (VII, 56).

"The deadly influence of egoism is connected not with a tendency to ascribe to oneself some importance, or even with making oneself a centre of life—for each individual is in some way a vital focus of the life-process—but in separating oneself from all others" (VII, 17).

Egoism was a prison, the walls of which had to be broken down, and, according to Soloviev, the natural power most capable of liberating an individual from this captivity was sexual love. In *The Meaning of Love* (1892), Soloviev stated that "The purpose of love is to vindicate and deliver individuality by destroying egoism" (VII, 16). Sexual love was to him the most dynamic of all forms of love; it was more revolutionary than maternal love or love for one's country, art or science; for it destroyed more radically than any other devotion the egoism of an individual by admitting into the very citadel of self-centredness a stranger—a stranger who has often nothing in common with the owner of the castle. Sexual love made this intruder master of the fortress. Once the walls of egoism were destroyed, the bewildered lover saw the world in an entirely new light. He began to realise its original glory and beauty, concealed hitherto by his self-centredness; he acquired the sense of the purpose of his existence; love opened to him the gates of eternal life.

These assertions led Soloviev to some of his most paradoxical statements. He insisted that the only real object of sexual love was the Divine Sophia; she contained the fullness of created life; she was the bearer of perfect beauty and harmony, and therefore she alone was the attraction which in reality drew and held each individual lover (VII, 47). But this Divine Sophia could be approached by an individual only with the help and through the medium of another individual, who appeared in the sight of the lover illuminated by celestial glory, and by becoming thus the centre of irresistible attraction he dragged him from the dark and gloomy prison of self-centredness out into the bright and colourful world of love and life in common. The lovers were thus made capable of contemplating the divine image in each other. Their mutual adoration was justified, for each created being was intended by God to be perfect; but the common mistake of lovers was to identify the *actual state* of the beloved with the ideal which has to be achieved, and this confusion led inevitably to deep disappointment, which often frustrated the beneficent effects of love.

Man, as the conscious representative of created life, had a task before him. He was not meant passively to contemplate the Divine Sophia; he was called actively to collaborate with God in restoring the fallen world to its original glory. This work could only be done gradually, by perfecting each individual manifestation of life, by attuning it to the preordained harmony. Every genuine lover dimly realised this task not only by admiring but also by wanting to help the beloved to become better and more beautiful. These efforts at improving one another seldom succeeded, for few were able to see that one could assist the perfection of another only by becoming more perfect oneself. But no one could make oneself perfect; if this task could be achieved by an individual unassisted by others, love would lose its purpose. But as man cannot grow into full life without love, so equally he cannot use properly, in his present state, the power of love given him for his assistance. "Man needs the Saviour" (VII, 42). This is the significant conclusion at which Soloviev arrived in the course of his study of the purpose of sexual love. "True love can never be satisfied till it sees the beloved delivered from the threat of death and decay, and reborn in perfect beauty" (IX, 231). And because love has no limits it cannot be satisfied with the eternal enjoyment of life by a few individuals alone. It asks for the final victory of harmony over destruction, of beauty over ugliness, of life over death, and this can be achieved only by means of the general resurrection and the transfiguration of the cosmos (VII, 52). Two human beings falling in love with each other start out on a road the final destination of which is the restoration of the world to its original purpose and beauty; but because most lovers fail to understand it, and see in love only personal enjoyment, they soon feel frustrated, and then they call the heavenly vision given them an illusion, and reduce the purpose of sexual love either to the satisfaction of the flesh, or to the establishment of a family with its chief object in the procreation of children.

Soloviev counted among the abuses of love not only sexual promiscuity, which reduced love to a physiological act, degrading man to the animal level, but also marriages in which social conventions and material interests took the place of love. All those who indulge in such degradations of the gift from above are heavily punished. They become dull and empty, unfit for eternal life.

Soloviev concluded his essay with the assertion that man's attitude to society, to the nation, and to the whole of mankind must be coloured by the emotions which he experienced in sexual love. Even man's attitude to nature ought to be radically changed, for the cosmos is a person who needs man's love to become transparent and obedient to the call of the Holy Spirit (VII, 59).

In his study of man's place in the life of the universe, Soloviev arrived at the conclusion that an individual can find the fulfilment of his personality through willingness to identify himself with the cosmic process, and believed that the same principle governed the life of nations. In a series of articles published later under the general title, *The National Question in Russia* (1883–91), Soloviev developed a consistent Christian interpretation of the meaning and value of nationality.

Each nation, like each individual, had, according to him, its special mission, but this did not mean that the greater the nation the more extensive were its rights over others; on the contrary, each nation could find its proper place in the life of mankind only through its service to the common cause. Egoism was as destructive for a nation as for an individual. Selfishness turned the positive force of nationality into evil nationalism (V, 13). "Nationalism in its extreme form destroys a nation, for it makes it an enemy of mankind, and mankind is always stronger than any one nation. Christianity saves the nations, for it helps them to transcend nationalism" (V, 83). Soloviev was particularly opposed to the view that moral laws were inapplicable to international relations. The nations were for him collective persons, and he insisted that "inhumanity in international relations, the policy of cannibalism, will eventually destroy the moral principles in personal and family life, and this is already seen in the whole Christian world" (V, 14). He believed that the only consistent point of view was the Christian one, for it asked an individual to sacrifice his selfishness for the sake of the nation, and a nation in the same way to serve mankind: "Christianity appealed to each and to all together to work for the same cause of universal salvation" (V, 14). In *The Justification of the Good*,[1] published in 1897, Soloviev developed fully his idea of the common task which mankind had to fulfil and which alone gave meaning to the life of individuals and nations. His main idea was that the individual could not be separated from society, since they formed one indissoluble whole.

"Society is the completed individual, and the individual is concentrated society" (204). "Each single individual possesses as such the potentiality of perfection, but by remaining isolated and limited an individual deprives himself of the real fullness of life, i.e. of perfection and infinity" (203). "The Kingdom of God

---

[1] An English translation by Nathalie Duddington was published in 1918, *The Justification of the Good*, by V. Soloviev, Constable. All further quotations referring to this work are made from that edition.

is both perfectly universal and perfectly individual. Each wants it for himself and for everyone, and is only able to obtain it together with others" (199). "The purpose of moral progress is not to create solidarity between each and all, for it already exists, but to make each and all aware of this solidarity . . . so that each should fulfil the common work as if it were his own" (204). It followed from this that the growth of each person could proceed only in close organic unity with the rest of mankind, and this meant that the right social organisation of society was of paramount importance to the salvation of each individual. "Only a perfect and all-embracing society can satisfy an individual, a complete submission to a limited society is degrading" (213). Soloviev was keenly aware that loyalty to the collectivity, the readiness to sacrifice oneself for its sake, could be the greatest moral danger, and result in social regress instead of progress, "for the degree of subordination of the individual to the society must correspond to the degree of subordination of society to the moral good" (260). This moral good he defined as "the principle of human dignity, or of the absolute worth of each individual in virtue of which society is determined as the inward and free harmony of all" (266). But this high ideal was out of the reach of sinful man. Society in its natural order, which had three stages of self-expression, the family, the nation and humanity, had to be despotic and use coercion against its disobedient members in order to overcome their egoism. This despotism was a necessary stage in the evolution of human collectivity. "In order to outgrow tyranny, mankind has first to experience it" (224). This gradual process of growth could, however, never bring man to a really satisfactory social order. The natural society, whatever was its political or religious constitution, has never been able to recognise the human rights of three classes of men: (a) enemies, and such were the majority of foreigners, (b) slaves, together with the destitute and helpless, and (c) criminals, including the rebels against the established social and political order (270). This high wall of national and social prejudices and hostility which made progress towards the realisation of the universal, harmonious and progressive order impossible, could be broken down only by Christianity. "When men of different nationality and class were spiritually united in worshipping a foreigner and a beggar . . . the Galilean who was executed as a criminal in the name of national and class interests—international wars, the rightlessness of the masses and the execution of criminals were inwardly undermined" (272). The road to a perfect society was open, but progress remained painfully uncertain, for "Christianity set before mankind a moral task and therefore a free one, and this is the reason why Christian progress is so slow" (275). Still, the Church had at last found the way out of the social impasse. She alone knew how to check the three main manifestations of evil in the collective life: hostility between different nations, between society and criminals and between different classes" (276).

Soloviev's demand for Christian action in international relations, for the humanisation of the criminal code, and for ending social inequality and exploitation, was novel to the Christians of his time, but it has been accepted by a large number of them in the twentieth century. He was a forerunner of the Œcumenical movement, for he was the first to make it clear that the efficacy of Church actions both in the social and the international spheres would depend on the restoration of Christian unity. The originality of Soloviev's thought consisted, however, not so much in his programme of reform as in the ultimate motives behind the measures he advocated. These were as striking in his own day as in ours, for they were based on a deep conviction that the ultimate object of the Christian social order was nothing less than the resurrection of the dead, and the transfiguration of the cosmos.

Every human work aimed potentially at that distant goal, but only in the light of faith in the Incarnation could men see it clearly. "Labour is interaction between men and the material world; it must secure to each and to all the necessary means of worthy existence, and is finally destined to transfigure and spiritualise material nature" (349). "Without loving nature for its own sake it is impossible to organise material life in a moral way" (347).

In order to achieve it, man must understand that the cosmos is a person "and must be cherished like the being whom one loves" (358).

But even the most satisfactory social order and the best and wisest use of natural gifts could never secure real happiness and harmony unless death, the last enemy, was conquered. Man could never be at home on earth till he felt free, and there could be no freedom so long as men, who wanted to live, were all condemned to death, their only consolation being that most of them did not know the hour when their end would come.

Any social order reconciled to death contained in it the seeds of disharmony and destruction, and therefore could never be perfect. Here Soloviev stood in irreconcilable opposition to all forms of the materialist Utopianism which promised its followers happiness and joy without attempting to face the grim reality of universal death.

"If we are indifferent to the future of our forefathers, we can have no motives for caring about the future of the new generations. If we can have no absolute moral solidarity with those who died, there can be no ground for such solidarity with those who certainly will die" (422). These words expressed in a forcible way some of the most significant views ever held by a Christian sociologist, and they reveal the integrity of Soloviev's belief that mankind is one body animated by the mutual love and solidarity of all its members. For Soloviev, the departed were truly alive; they still had their share in the life and work of humanity. "The departed living in the memory of the past have also a hidden existence in the present which will become manifest in the future. They have both future and actuality" (422). "The indissoluble moral bond between generations can be found only in their common task of preparing for the revelation of the Kingdom of God and for universal resurrection" (433).

This grandiose vision of the final unity and reconciliation of mankind, accompanied by the glorification of the whole cosmos, could be realised by men only under the guidance of the Church, for she was the ladder leading from earth to heaven. "Man lives in three different spheres: this world, the Kingdom of God and the Church which binds them together" (432).

"Perfect unity and holiness is in God; divisions and sin in the worldly humanity; union and consecration in the Church . . . but in order to unite and consecrate, the Church itself must be one and holy" (134).

The Church was the only body which could direct the efforts of mankind towards the final goal of universal salvation. She alone was able to organise properly the labours of individuals and provide each man with the moral resources necessary for his struggle against sin and death. She was the society to which a man could give his full allegiance without degrading himself by serving an unworthy object. But in order to fulfil all these tasks the Church had to be truly One, Holy, Catholic and Apostolic, embracing everybody, caring for everyone, and especially never forgetting its departed members; for love required their restoration to the fullness of life.

"The Catholicity of the Church—the fundamental form of the moral organisation of humanity—is the conscious and intentional unity between all the members of the universal body in relation to one absolute purpose of existence and unity, accompanied by complete division of gifts and services" (435).

"Only in the Church was man made truly free, for only Christianity had a hope of the conquest of death" (436).

"Only in the Church was genuine equality achievable, for it initiates each into the wholeness of the Divine life, and communicates to each the absolute content of life" (437).

Such was the daring conception of the place of the Christian religion in the evolution of mankind developed by Soloviev. The importance which he attributed to it did not make him indifferent to other forms of collective life. He particularly emphasised the significance of the State.

The Church was for him organised piety; "the State was organised pity" (449). Its purpose was to defend the weak and the oppressed, and to prevent evil doers from harming those who could not defend themselves. Soloviev followed the tradition of Russian Christianity in resolutely opposing capital punishment. His attitude to the criminal was the outcome of his conception of the organic unity of mankind. "Punishment as intimidating revenge is immoral. Moral principles require resistance to crimes as an act of active pity limiting the external expressions of evil will, not only for the sake of the victims, but also in the interest of the criminal himself" (322). "A criminal has a right to reformation; society must provide for him the conditions most favourable for self-reform" (325).

Soloviev felt acutely that internal harmony was unachievable in the Christian State as long as hate and revenge dominated the attitude to wrongdoers. He argued that if intimidation was justified, then the use of torture must be approved also. Thus Soloviev defined the Christian State as an instrument for the establishing of the kingdom of righteousness on earth, but its function was distinct from that of the Church. He gave the following description of their interrelation: "The State recognises the supreme spiritual authority of the Universal Church which indicates the general direction of the goodwill of mankind, and the final purpose of its historical activity. The Church leaves to the State full power to bring lawful worldly interests into conformity with this supreme will, and to harmonise political relations and actions with the requirements of this supreme purpose. The Church must have no power of compulsion, and the power of compulsion exercised by the State must have nothing to do with the domain of religion" (459). "The rule of true progress is this,

K

that the State should interfere as little as possible with the inner moral life of man, and at the same time should as securely and as widely as possible ensure the external conditions of his worthy existence and moral development" (459).

Both the Church and the State had their own responsibility, and only in close co-operation with each other could they discharge them successfully. But what would happen if they disagreed, and could not trace the line of demarcation of their spheres of action?

Soloviev's solution of this crucial question was the appeal to the authority of the prophets as the highest expression of the Christian conscience. "The true prophet is a social worker who, since he neither fears nor submits to anything external, represents absolute freedom" (468). "The supreme authority and power are given by the grace of God; the true freedom man must deserve for himself by self-renunciation" (469). Priesthood and kingship were institutions, representatives of which were called to their offices by the will of God and by the consent of other men; a prophet was a free agent, controlled neither by the hierarchy nor by State officials; he was outside their domain, and therefore he alone was able to reconcile them and to act as their judge.

Such was Soloviev's vision of the organisation of Christian mankind as a free theocracy which would ensure to each and all the joy and bliss of communion with the Holy Spirit, and make man's sojourn on this earth the preparation for Paradise.

For Soloviev this vision was not merely poetic imagination, but a scientific forecast of the course of evolution. He could never separate body and spirit nor discuss religion without mentioning its implications for the physical aspects of life. This explains his persistent emphasis on the resurrection of the dead and the transfiguration of the cosmos as the only satisfactory objects of the corporate efforts of the human race.

Soloviev's attitude to theocracy, therefore, was not that of a theoretical discussion of its possibility; he was interested in the study of concrete examples of God's methods of dealing with mankind. Theocracy could be proved only historically, and this task Soloviev achieved in his monumental work, *The History and Future of Theocracy* (1885–97). The greater part of it consists of an interpretation of the Old Testament. He described its meaning as the gradual preparation of mankind for the Incarnation. This training had two aspects: it was a moral contest between God and man during which the human will was tested, and at the same time it was a process of breeding a new race distinct both in spirit and flesh from all other nations. Soloviev was profoundly absorbed in the destiny of the Jews—the people of the Incarnation, who alone had been capable of entering into a covenant with the Maker of the Universe.

Soloviev believed that the Jews were the only people who were free from two great religious perversions—that of longing to be absorbed in God conceived as being beyond men's comprehension, and outside any moral law, and that of attempting to shape gods according to the will of men. The most typical example of the first attitude was Hindu pantheism, with its Nirvana. The most typical example of the second was provided by Rome, where the State assumed control over the gods, and by its own decrees added to their numbers and dethroned those who were no longer approved by the Eternal City. The Jews were able to combine a belief in the Personal God who was the absolute Master of the Universe with an intense awareness of God's activity in and upon the life of humanity. They possessed three theocratic virtues essential for the success of mankind's co-operation with its Creator. The first was the ardour of their faith, their readiness to dedicate their entire lives to a religious cause The second was their highly developed sense of personality, their activism, the conviction of their own importance, which they extended to their families and their whole race. And, thirdly, their materialism, which was expressed in their sensuality and in their aptitude for commerce and finance (IV, 432–3).

They were a vigorous, hard and difficult race, but they were not, like Oriental people, passive and submissive to Divinity, nor, like the Greeks and Romans, self-centred, worshipping themselves under the image of gods of their own creation.

"The Holy and Mighty God desired as the partner of His covenant a strong man who aspired to holiness, and such a man was the Jew" (IV, 145). The Old Covenant was concluded with a people who were ready to obey Divine commandments, but only if thereby they received some personal benefit. They were capable of defending their legitimate rights, and, if necessary, even of resisting their Maker. Their name, "Israel," described them as the Strugglers against the Almighty.

The ultimate object of the covenant between God and the Jews was to prepare the way for the Incarnation. Jewish materialism was most essential for the success of the Divine plan.

"The whole religious history of the Jews aimed at preparing

for the God of Israel not only holy souls, but also holy bodies"
(IV, 149). A Jew refused to divide spirit from matter; the Old
Covenant was as much concerned with moral laws as with
questions of proper food, dress, vessels and other material aspects
of human life. Only people who acutely felt the importance of
flesh could provide God with flesh sufficiently pure and holy for
the Incarnation. The Old Testament was, for Soloviev, the story
of a race which in the person of the Virgin Mary finally responded
positively to the challenge of the Annunciation. The Jews had
delivered mankind alike from the Western worship of deified
men and from the Eastern cult of inhuman deities. These two
principal aberrations in the human search for God vanished in
the light of the one true God-man, Jesus Christ, the Saviour, not
of men alone, but of the whole creation.

"Christianity," wrote Soloviev, "is the revelation of a perfect
God in a perfect man" (IV, 30). Man could never reach perfection
through his own efforts, and because God required in him a companion capable of rendering a free and intelligent love for his
Creator, the Incarnation became necessary. The Church, which
was the fruit of the Incarnation, provided man with all the conditions essential for his training to be God's collaborator. The
egoism of individuals, the selfishness of families and classes, the lust
for power displayed by nations were checked, and eventually
cured, in the œcumenical fellowship of the Christian Church.
All human beings, individually and collectively, could find their
fulfilment in the world-wide and free brotherhood of those who
believed in the Incarnation. Concord and love among the members
of the Church was indispensable for the success of their mission,
which consisted in proclaiming to the world that perfect unity
between Divine and human was possible. This was exactly the
point which was constantly denied by heresies. In Eastern and
Western Christendom alike these heresies tended to explain away
the reality of God-manhood embodied once and for ever in the
Person of Jesus Christ. In the East the natural tendency of the
human mind led to the exaltation of the Divine at the expense of
the human; in the West, on the contrary, to the assertion of man
as a self-sufficient and independent being.
    The greatest of all Eastern heresies was Islam which recalled
a large body of Christians to the oriental belief in an inhuman

God (IV, 43). In the West, the godless man reappeared on the scene under the auspices of the rationalism and secularism of modern civilisation. Both the Orthodox and the Latin Churches have successfully defended the faith in the Incarnation against the attacks of the heretics. The Eastern Christians at the time of the Œcumenical Councils were particularly exposed to the fury of these assaults, but they stood firm against them all, including the last great heresy of iconoclasm, which, by insisting that Christ cannot be represented in pictorial form, strove surreptitiously once more to create an impassable gulf between the Divine and the human. But neither the Eastern nor the Western Churches had been able to do more than defend the orthodoxy of the faith. Their attempts to Christianise the social and political life of the nations had failed. Their members were unable to resist the pressure of national and racial pride. Both sides lacked love and understanding of each other (IV, 61), hence the inevitability of their schism. It came as a relief to many who felt that at last they could give themselves freely to their natural inclinations. Both Churches went their own way, enjoying the full use of their gifts, but the penalty of their separation was a one-sided development which turned their very virtues into vices: "the humility and patience of the Eastern people degenerated into submissiveness and passive resignation; the courage and activism of the Western man changed into arrogance and pride" (IV, 21). The split within the Church was an open violation of the very principle of its religion. This inconsistency between teaching and practice provided the Mahometans in the East and the secularists in the West with deadly weapons against Christianity. The Church, being an organic body, could live and act healthily only when all its organs were co-ordinated; the glory of the Christian fellowship was the harmony of diverse gifts, a free co-operation between different groups and nations. Only a truly œcumenical Church, the embodiment of a free theocracy, could Christianise the world and present with authority the truth of the Incarnation. Because Christians lost their unity, their progress was retarded, and they suffered one defeat after another.

By emphasising the vital importance of Christian reunion, both for the West and for the East, Soloviev gradually departed from the traditional position held by the Orthodox. He could not treat the Western Christians any longer as apostates from the truth. He frankly acknowledged that the Eastern Church had paid as dearly for the split as Western Christendom, and that both parties

were equally guilty of the sin of schism. He based his hope for
Christian victory, not on the triumph of Eastern Orthodoxy,
but on the reintegration of the whole Church, resulting from the
restoration of communion between the Eastern and Western
streams of tradition.

Like Khomiakov and Dostoevsky, Soloviev was fascinated by
the problem of Russia and of her relation to Europe. He started
as a Slavophil, and under Dostoevsky's influence he taught that
"Russia has a religious calling of world-wide significance and
that the poverty and humiliation of her people are the signs of
their special pre-election" (II, 323). He believed that Russia was
destined to inaugurate a new epoch in the history of mankind,
and to achieve the synthesis between Europe and Asia. At first,
like the rest of the Slavophils, he saw in the Orthodox Church
the force which could bring about this reconciliation, but later
changed his mind. He entered into long and bitter controversy
with his former friends, accusing them of obscurantism and narrow
nationalism. Soloviev continued, even after his break with the
Slavophils, to preach that Moscow was the third Rome, but he
offered an entirely novel interpretation of this traditional belief.
He taught that the major calamity of Christian history was the
rivalry between Rome and Constantinople, and that Moscow had
a mission to reconcile these two ancient foes. Only by success in
this could she claim to be the third and last Rome, otherwise she
would be nothing more than a poor copy of the second Rome,
and, like Constantinople, would remain a centre of strife and
hostility against the Latin world (V, 22).

The failure of the Moscow Tsardom, according to him, was due to
its suspicion of Western Christendom. The new Russia started by
Peter the Great had to embrace both the Eastern and Western
Christian traditions. Soloviev's hopes that Russia was called to
take a leading part in the future destiny of Christian civilisation
were based on two events of Russian history: the invitation to
the Vikings in the ninth century to come and rule over the people
of Novgorod and Peter's reforms in the eighteenth century. On
both occasions the Russians, according to Soloviev, voluntarily
abandoned their national exclusiveness, conquered their pride, and
as a result enriched their life and achieved objects which were
out of their grasp whilst they remained in the state of isolation

(V, 29). Only a great people could act thus. Soloviev's belief that individuals and nations could grow only if they overcame their self-centredness was confirmed by the example of his own country.

In opposition to the Slavophils, who treated Peter the Great's reforms as a national calamity, Soloviev declared that "Peter mercilessly broke down the hard crust of nationalistic exclusiveness, which contained the seed of original Russian culture, and boldly threw this seed into the soil of universal European history" (V. 20). This contact between Russia and the West, however, Soloviev contended, was limited to the externals of civilisation, but it was now time for Russia to accomplish her mission and establish concord and mutual understanding between the Christian East and the Christian West. "Without such reconciliation, Russia cannot serve God's cause on earth. Russia's mission is a Christian mission and Russian policy must be a Christian policy" (V, 20).

The geographical expansion of the Empire placed before the Russian people the responsible task of solving three of the most difficult problems of modern Europe. These were the Polish, the Balkan and the Jewish questions, and "they were all closely bound together, for they were different aspects of the same great conflict between the East and the West which has marked the whole history of mankind" (V, 17). No one of them could be solved without the restoration of Church unity. Soloviev was aware how deeply rooted was the hostility between the Eastern and the Latin Christians. The case of Poland was an example. The Roman Catholic Poles were more easily reconciled to the rule of Protestant Germans, which meant complete denationalisation to them, than to their incorporation into the Russian Empire, though under the Russian Eagle they were able to preserve their nationality and religion. They felt it more humiliating to be controlled by the barbaric Eastern Christians, who were outside the commonwealth of Western Christendom, than to be subjugated to the "cultured" Germans (IV, 14–15). The Christian West, both Catholic and Protestant, was always ready to support Poland against Russia, for by so doing it was merely continuing the old conflict between Rome and Constantinople, which revealed all its bitterness at the time when the Crusaders attacked the Byzantine Empire in the twelfth century. Soloviev wrote: "The West destroyed the second Rome, Constantinople" and was equally irreconcilably hostile to the third Rome, the Empire of Russia (IV, 16). But in spite of this centuries-long conflict, Soloviev believed in the possibility of a new understanding with the Roman

Church, and he called the Russians to set the example of brotherly love and forgiveness in order to make possible the œcumenical fellowship of all Christians. Soloviev was hurt by the indifference of the Westernisers and by the animosity of the Slavophils. Both camps of the Russian educated classes rejected his appeals for reconciliation. His attacks on Russia and his negotiations with Rome were his reactions to this hostile reception. But even during the time when he was the most ardent advocate of the Roman primacy, he retained much of his original Slavophil outlook, for he persisted in his belief that Russia alone was able to make an act of Christian forgiveness, and thus take the leadership in the reunion of the Church. He never expected that Rome would have faith and love enough to make the decisive move.

Soloviev was an optimist; he entertained hopes that mankind would realise wherein lies the source of its happiness and power, and would direct its efforts, not towards wars and destruction, but towards the conquest of egoism, discord and death. He also trusted Christians with the sense of understanding that they must bring to an end their divisions, if they wanted to be the leaders in social regeneration. But in spite of his optimism, in spite of his plans and activities, he remained also aware that hope and trust could not amount to certainty. The vision of a catastrophe which would shatter into pieces Christian civilisation and bring humanity into the abyss of suffering and oppression was always present in his mind. This acute awareness of impending danger was probably one of the reasons for Soloviev's inexhaustible energy and for the persistent but unheeded warnings he addressed to his contemporaries.

Towards the very end of his life, Soloviev passed through his last and greatest crisis. He suddenly realised that the truth might lie, not in his golden hopes, but in the terrifying vision of the triumph of evil which had haunted him from his youth. He was obliged to accept the grim fact that the powers of darkness were stronger than he had supposed, that the unity of the Church for which he had worked and prayed might come under very different conditions from those he so eloquently postulated.

Soloviev's last work, the *Three Conversations*, still prophesied the reunion of Christendom, but this time he foresaw its coming, not as the result of the solemn reconciliation between the Pope and the Orthodox Emperor, but under the pressure of the universal rule of anti-Christian totalitarianism.

The *Three Conversations* recount a private discussion in which a politician, a pacifist, a general, a society lady and a Christian voicing Soloviev's point of view expressed their various opinions on war, progress and Christianity. At the end of it one of them reads to the rest a manuscript containing a prophetic description of the final events of human history. It seldom happens that attempts to penetrate the mystery of the future are crowned with success. They suffer usually either from being too vague or from being overcharged with details, few of which turn out to be true. Soloviev's last book is different. A spirit of tension permeates its pages. It reads like genuine prophecy, not mere literary apocalyptic. The vision seems to have imposed itself upon the seer and constrained him to describe it, in spite of the fact that it nullified the theories which he had previously expounded with such zeal and conviction.

The picture of Antichrist is so powerfully drawn, with all its parts so coherent and yet often so unexpected, that nothing could be added or taken away. The man who was made the vessel of this strange revelation could continue his normal life no longer. It was not by chance, therefore, that Soloviev died from utter mental and physical exhaustion after he had written his prophetic book. The story of the Antichrist is available in two English translations,[1] and there is no need to repeat it here. Its most important feature is the entirely new presentation of the final conflict between the Christian and anti-Christian forces. Traditionally the last and strongest enemy of the Church has been represented as a hateful and cruel tyrant, who, by means of bloody persecution, tries to stamp out the Christian religion. Soloviev's Antichrist is a very different person; he is the greatest benefactor of mankind; he introduces enlightened social reforms; he is the first man to establish universal peace and to abolish want together with social and racial antagonisms. He is a remarkable ruler inspired by noble ideas, who accepts the existence of God, but comes to save mankind, not in the Name of the Incarnate Lord, but in his own. He is met everywhere with overwhelming enthusiasm, and even the majority of Christians accept the enlightened leadership of the universal dictator. The representatives of the Church argue that "if the contents of his books are impregnated with the truly Christian spirit of effective love and universal benevolence, what is there left to wish for?" (159).

[1] *War and Christianity*, with an Introduction by S. Graham, Constable, London, 1915. *War, Progress and the End of History*, with a Biographical Note by Dr. H. Wright, London University Press, 1915. The quotations in this book are from S. Graham's edition.

Elected as the President of the United States of Europe, he issues a manifesto starting with the words: "Peoples of the earth, my peace I give to you" (161), and he fulfils his promise. His social reforms are equally successful, and "everyone began to receive in proportion to his ability, and according to his labour and merits" (162). The great ruler, though not belonging to any Church, is benevolent towards the Christians, who at that time form only a small minority. To assist them, he convokes a world conference of Christian Churches in Jerusalem. There, in a magnificent new hall, he offers various privileges to Christians, on condition that the representatives of all confessions will recognise him as their "sole protector and defender" (172). A large number of Christians gladly consent to this request, but a small minority, at the head of which stand Pope Peter II, John, the Russian Elder, the spokesman of the Eastern Church, and the learned German professor, Ernst Pauli, the leader of the Protestants, refuse such a recognition till they shall hear from the world's dictator his confession of faith in Jesus Christ, the Son of God.

This request provokes a drastic change in the hitherto patronising attitude of the superman towards the Christians. The persecution is launched which brings together the faithful remnant of those who, though belonging to different confessions, firmly profess their belief in the Incarnation. After the sudden death of Elder John, who was the first to recognise in the social reformer Christ's final adversary, the Antichrist, and of Pope Peter, who excommunicated the impostor, the leadership of the Church fell into the hands of Professor Pauli, who leads the faithful few into the desert and "there, after the restoration to life of Pope Peter and the Elder John, in the darkness of the night on a high and lonely place was accomplished the Union of the Churches" (184).

But this was not the beginning of a new and better epoch; it was the end of the history of mankind, "for the darkness was suddenly lightened by a bright splendour, and there appeared a great wonder in heaven: a Woman clothed in the sun, with the moon under her feet and a crown of twelve stars on her head" (184).

So ended the manuscript, and this was also the end of Soloviev's life. He had accomplished the work committed to him. He had recognised at last the full meaning of Hagia Sophia, the Divine Glory of the Cosmos, which, under the veil of the eternal feminine, was revealed to him for the first time when he was a boy of nine years old. All his life he remained faithful to this vision, and all the gifts he received from God he gave to the service of this great cause.

As a man he was often fallible in his judgments; his passions led him astray, and many a time in the turmoils and tensions of daily life he could not clearly see the face of the Heavenly Beloved. But his mistakes were only those incidental to human frailty and weakness, and Soloviev never doubted the reality of his calling. He died as he had lived, a man dedicated to the service of God, a genuine prophet of His coming Kingdom. He hoped all his life that mankind would repent of its sins of selfishness and pride, and voluntarily submit to the gentle yoke of Christ, which brings with it happiness and freedom. But on the threshold of the new century he suddenly realised all the improbability of his hopes, and he had the courage to face this revelation, but he had no strength to live under its crushing weight.

Chapter Five

THE FUTURE OF CHRISTIAN CIVILISATION

K<small>HOMIAKOV</small>, Dostoevsky and Soloviev belong to different generations. They were unlike in mentality and temperament, and yet they arrived at the same conclusions about the destiny of Europe and of their own country. They were able, with a truly prophetic insight, to foretell the crisis of Christian civilisation, and the leading part which Russia would take in these events. Beneath the humanistic trust in scientific progress, they discerned the sinister signs of decay and disintegration. Amidst the acclamation of the era of enlightenment and liberalism they sounded a note of warning. They predicted the outburst of dark and irrational passions, and the advent of enslavement and oppression on an unprecedented scale. They foretold the flare-up of religious persecution, the deification of the secularised State, and the willing surrender of intellectual and political freedom by the bewildered and de-Christianised masses of Europe. Their warnings were dismissed by the confident and matter-of-fact men of the nineteenth century as the words of eccentrics, who lived in a world of fantasy without contact with the realities of daily life. And yet it was not the practical man of the nineteenth century who proved, after all, to be right. The queer Russian writers had a better grasp than he of things to come. They stood on firm ground, whilst the liberals and the agnostics built their theories and expectations on shifting sand. These Russian thinkers were outstanding students of human nature. They knew man infinitely better than most of their contemporaries and many of the leaders of to-day. They were able to penetrate into those dark corners of the human soul which have a decisive influence, especially in times of anxiety and crisis, and this deep understanding of man enabled these Russians to predict the course of events with surprising accuracy.

They derived their knowledge not from books or lecture halls, but from their membership of the Orthodox Church. The ancient wisdom of Eastern Christianity provided them with the explanation of the purpose of man's existence; it helped them to interpret the conflict between good and evil, and to disentangle the meaning of suffering and freedom, these two greatest mysteries of human life. The Orthodox Church, so often described in the West as obsolete and superstitious, was the tutor and guide of these three great Russians. They learned from her how to approach the perplexing social problems of the scientific age, and how to understand the modern man. They were certain that a human being could not be satisfied with material progress only, that behind the patronising indifference to religion, prevalent in their time, there was a growing resentment against God, and that mankind stood on the eve of an open rebellion against its Creator. They were aware that the Christian nations could not live indefinitely in a state of compromise and indecision, and that sooner or later they would face a choice between a radical denial of Christianity, and the integral acceptance of its teaching. They were all three convinced that the fundamental cause of unrest and instability in modern Europe had to be sought, not only in the events of the last four centuries, but also in those remote years when the foundations of Western civilisation were laid. In this respect they differed from those Christian thinkers who have explained the present crisis as the consequence of social and economic changes brought about by the machine age, and sought remedies in the re-establishment of a Christian order not unlike that which collapsed in the West at the time of the Reformation.

Khomiakov, Dostoevsky and Soloviev were more radical. They believed that the defects of Christian civilisation were so serious that they required more drastic changes. The root of its failure, according to them, was the confusion as to the nature of the Church, which distorted the thought and action of the majority of Christians.

The men who built up the imposing edifice of European civilisation had failed to grasp all the implications of the Incarnation. They were either unable or unwilling to face its full challenge, and therefore they produced an order which was an outcome of compromise between Christianity and Roman paganism. European civilisation lacked consistency and therefore it was bound to collapse. According to the Russian teachers the Church was the instrument for the overthrow of sin and death; Christianity was the power capable of transfiguring the earth and the whole of nature. Christians were called to take full responsibility in the accomplishment of this task. They were drawn together into the Eucharistic fellowship composed of men and

women of all races and nations under no other law but the law
of love, no other master but God Himself. The Church was a free
theocracy, and only as such could she be the proper channel for
the operation of the Holy Spirit, who alone was able to regenerate men, beasts and plants. After the recognition of the
Church by the Empire and the influx of mass converts, the
members of the Church became frankly afraid; they felt staggered
and overwhelmed by the task assigned to them, and their reaction
was to alter the constitution of the Church, changing it into
a powerful institution, enshrining Christian truth and yet deliberately avoiding that unique type of fellowship life which
was experienced by its early members. There have been many
explanations offered of the reasons which induced the Christians
to give up their original freedom, and to accept the forms of
Church life modelled in accordance with the pattern of the Empire.
The Russian writers were familiar with the facts, but they were
unwilling to accept the process as the normal and inevitable
evolution of the Church organism. They believed that the true
motive behind these changes was the fear of sinful men to face
the Living God. The life of the early Church was based on the
direct rule of the Holy Spirit. Every member had to submit his
thoughts and actions to close examination by the Christian community, to stand daily under its judgment and to accept its discipline. It required the same act of faith as shown by Peter when
he walked on the water, and it proved to be too much for the
masses of new converts. They were not used to so close a fellowship with God the Almighty, they had no confidence in their
newly acquired freedom, and they sought therefore to shift from
their shoulders the burden of responsibility for partnership with
the Creator in the redemption of the world.

   The bulk of Christians preferred to entrust their safety to the
protection of a well-constructed boat rather than risk other less
usual ways of crossing the sea of life. Thus the Church was
gradually transformed and rebuilt on the pattern familiar to the
majority of its members. They shaped it in conformity with
the universal organisation of Imperial Rome, displaying much
devotion, efficiency, and sacrifice in the task. They thought that
they had created a perfect instrument for the promotion of their
religion. Laws and rules were promulgated, salutary discipline
was imposed, necessary punishment of the slack and reluctant was
inflicted, an army of well-trained officials was provided, and the
grandiose structure was crowned by a single head, obedience to

whom was the guarantee of the unity and stability of the whole edifice.

But the magnificent temple had one defect. Its plan did not correspond with the intention of the Master-Builder. The Church was not called to govern the world, but to transform it from within, but this it could not achieve. It failed to establish a Christian order; on the contrary, it brought forth fruits which were obviously not intended by its Founder. Prisons and scaffolds were erected where people were tortured and executed in the name of the Redeemer of the world. Wars were waged for the sake of the Prince of Peace. Cruelty and injustice were committed on the strength of the Gospel texts. The Church grew richer and stronger, but it was not the kind of strength and wealth promised by the Incarnate Lord to His disciples. Members of the Church realised the danger. Many attempts at reformation were made, but none of them was daring enough to go to the root of the trouble; they all tried to remedy the external consequence of disobedience without touching the evil itself. Eventually the visible unity of the Church was lost, for the doctors could not agree upon the cure. The schisms, however, did not improve matters. Besides a Church shaped like an Empire, the Christians produced Churches organised like city republics, private associations and clubs. A large variety of ecclesiastical governments has been invented, but none of them has secured the revival of Christianity. On the contrary, the increasing animosity between Church members weakened their fellowship with the Holy Spirit and further undermined the vitality of the Body.

The most serious indictment brought by the Russian writers against Western Christendom was that its leaders and rank and file substituted for the true task of the Church their own definition of its purpose. The Church became for many an institution for the maintenance of good morals, social justice and better education. The Christians transferred the Biblical promises of the victory of good over evil from this world to the future, and interpreted salvation as the release of the soul from the burden and responsibility of the earthly struggle. The abandoning of the original claims was inevitable, for the Christians, by altering the constitution of the Church, had deprived themselves of all chances of reaching the true goal. It was no wonder, therefore, that when they tried to use the language of the Apostles their words sounded hollow and unconvincing in their mouth. Divided and hostile, ridden by fears, prejudices and suspicions, they were unfit to become the vehicles of the Holy Spirit. Neither they themselves, nor the unbelieving world, took seriously their claims to be the messengers of Christ's Kingdom.

It was only to be expected, therefore, that the Christians were obliged to tone down their preaching and to give up those parts of it which are particularly challenging and incredible to the human mind unenlightened by faith in the Incarnation. Instead of proclaiming that the Church has the power to heal the sick, to cure sin, to destroy corruption and death, and to reveal the original beauty and glory of the Creation, the Christians have made strenuous efforts to convince the unbelieving world that their main concern is moral improvement and that there is nothing unreasonable and extravagant in their teaching, nothing that is not already contained in the ideals of enlightened humanism.

But the more modest the claims of the Church, the more practical its programme, the less it makes an appeal to mankind, which needs a cure for sin and not an edifying discourse on the advantages of decent behaviour and better education. A Church which can only offer social service is superfluous in the modern world where the State with the greatest efficiency and power can tackle the question of popular instruction and the raising of the economic standard among the masses.

Once the Church had abandoned its own domain and had begun to imitate the State, it embarked upon a course of capitulation— the State was bound to be the stronger of the two, for it stood on its own ground, whilst the Church was but an intruder.

The Russian prophets foresaw the apostasy of those Christians who had lost the understanding of their own mission, and they predicted that as long as the Church did not press its claim to be able to establish heaven upon earth, the leaders of secular Utopianism would step in and by using that very claim would inflame the imagination of millions of lapsed Christians.

This prediction has been confirmed in our own time: for one of its most paradoxical features is the whole-hearted belief of the former sceptics and agnostics in the most extravagant promises made by the totalitarian States to establish here on earth the millennium of righteousness, prosperity and freedom. Those who have discarded the Church preaching of the redemption of the world from sin have eagerly accepted the same message when it has been presented to them under the banners of anti-Christian secularism.

The Russian writers were certain that the conflict between

the Church and secularised State was inevitable, and that the
clash would be exceptionally bitter. They believed at the same
time that the victory of Christianity could be achieved neither
by compromise nor by further withdrawal, but only by bold
proclamation of the full Christian truth accompanied by the
liberation of the Church from all vestiges of its long association
with State, and its inevitable reliance upon compulsion.

The most important part of their writings are the positive
measures suggested by them for the revival of Christianity. The
first steps in the right direction, according to them, had to be the
recovery by men of their true place in the cosmos. Before
Christianity human beings were often terrified by Nature, and
pre-Christian religions bear striking proofs of the deep-seated
feeling of terror and insecurity. The faith in the Incarnation
liberated men from this bondage, and opened wide the door to
the knowledge of physical laws, and eventually helped mankind
to establish control over Nature. But the Church, because it lost
sight of its true purpose, failed to teach men the sacramental meaning of science and technical progress. Instead of treating them as
the extension of the Incarnation, and as the proof that God has
committed to men the task of making this earth sinless and perfect,
the members of the Church surrendered these powerful weapons
to the charge of secularised forces, and, in the hands of unscrupulous
leaders, they became, not means of salvation, but instruments for
a base and greedy exploitation of men, animals and plants, and
of all physical resources.

The destructive consequences of this misuse soon became
apparent. Men began to behave towards the earth as intruders,
degrading her and treating her as the means of their selfish enjoyment; they were intoxicated by their suddenly acquired power,
and yet uncertain about their ultimate future, fearful of the thought
that the true master might one day ask them to give an account
of their conduct. Fear makes people cruel; the modern man is
no longer terrified of Nature, but he is far from being really at
home on the earth. He is frightened of life, of himself, of others,
and therefore he tortures Nature and destroys his fellow creatures.

No real advance in Christian civilisation is possible till the
members of the Church show to the rest of mankind the example
of love and respect for the earth, and explain the true goal of
technical progress. Only then will men realise their unity and
interdependence, restore harmony between them and the animals
and plants, and assign true dignity to their labours. Only as

L

participants in the Eucharistic Fellowship, freely obeying the call
of the Holy Spirit, can they overcome their fears and sense of
insecurity and dedicate all their creative forces to the accomplishment of their final task, the transformation of the earth into God's
Kingdom.

The Russian writers connected this revival of Christianity with
the special mission of the Russian Church, which, according to
them, was called to reveal to the rest of Christendom the true
meaning of free theocracy. This part of the prophecy sounds the
least convincing. The events of the Russian Revolution seem to
deny the possibility of any help coming from the Russian Church.
The fierce anti-Christian campaign launched by the Communists
in the U.S.S.R. suggests that the Russians either lost, or never
had, that devotion to Christ about which all three Russian thinkers
wrote so eloquently.

The impression of the utter collapse of religion in Russia is
not confirmed by facts, however. On the contrary, a careful study
of the conflict between the Christians and the Godless supports all
the main contentions made by the Russian prophets. For they
predicted that though Europe would formulate the atheistic
doctrine, yet the Russian imitators of the West would be the
first to put it into practice. They were confident at the same time
that the Russian Church, the least affected by institutionalism and
secularism, would present the strongest opposition to the militant
atheism of the deified State. These expectations proved to be
right. It was not in Italy, the home of the Roman Catholic Church,
nor in Germany, the centre of Christian learning and the
Reformation, but in remote Russia that the greatest battle in
history between those who believe and those who deny the
existence of God took place, and was fought to a finish. The
Communist Revolution in Russia has been a decisive event in the
religious history of mankind. Since the beginning of Christianity
nothing has affected more profoundly man's attitude to God than the
anti-God campaign launched by the leaders of the Communist Party.

It is highly significant that this radical religious revolution was
inspired by the doctrine of Karl Marx. He was both a German
scholar and a Jewish prophet. As a German, he represented the
last word in European secularism, with its conviction that only
material things matter, and that science and planning would
eventually solve all the problems of human life. But he was more
than a learned economist absorbed in statistics; he was also a fiery
Jew with the drive of an Old Testament prophet, but a rebel

prophet, who cried out against the Almighty in anger and indignation because the world, as he saw it, was lacking in justice and mercy and was full of iniquity and sin. Karl Marx believed in the Messiah as only a Jew can believe in Him, but his Messiah was no longer God's Anointed, but a body of people, the lowest and poorest class of mankind, who did the hardest work and received the least remuneration for it. He proclaimed the coming of a collective Messiah, represented by the proletariat. With a fervent faith, he ascribed to the working classes all the· Biblical promises, and awaited the day when the proletariat would rise from its stupor and smash with its mighty arm all its treacherous enemies, and establish here on earth the messianic kingdom of righteousness and brotherly love.

The apocalyptic elements of Marx's thought had no logical connection with his scientific theories. The world of economic necessity had no bridge leading into the realm of equality and freedom. Marx taught that only through some great crisis could mankind ever reach the state of heavenly bliss, and this crisis he identified with the outbreak of the worldwide Revolution which by fire and blood would purify and regenerate corrupted human nature, and release it from its servitude to greed and fear. The doctrine of Communism reflects the two sides of the personality of its founder. On the one hand, it obediently follows the materialistic trend of European thought, denies human freedom, accepts selfishness as the prime motive behind all human actions, treats men as parts of a vast mechanism, describing their conduct and feelings as entirely conditioned by economic necessity. But, on the other hand, Marxian teaching represents the most violent protest against the lack of belief and against the egotism and disintegration of the European people. It is a revolt against the enslavement of men to matter, and a call for the restoration of human dignity and freedom. Marxian Communism is an unusual mixture of science and prophecy, and this is the source of its driving power, for it appeals both to the intellect and to the emotions, and touches the deep, religious springs of the human soul.

Karl Marx was born and brought up in an atmosphere of Christian culture, but he did not belong to it. He was a stranger who felt with great acuteness the failures and inconsistency of Western civilisation, for he had no experience of the healing and redemptive forces within the Christian Church. He was therefore more ready to smash it into pieces than were those men whose fathers and forefathers so lovingly and patiently had built up the

Western Christian world. The judgment upon Europe was pronounced by a Jewish seer, and the first country which followed
his lead was Russia. Many and diverse causes secured the victory
of Communism there. The most important among them was the
religious affinity between Marxism and the Russian outlook.
They met each other on Biblical ground. Economically Russia
was the land least suited for the Communist experiment, but
spiritually it was the only one which was ready to make the plunge
into a new world. Its people were neither disillusioned nor resigned
to their fate; they were still believers who accepted the possibility
of the redemption of the universe, and they, like Marx, were
eager to experiment on a worldwide scale.

Marxian Communism promises the final elimination of evil
from the life of creation, it prophesies the restoration of brotherhood among men, it expects Nature to supply mankind with all
the produce needed for its existence. All these ideas were familiar
to the Russian mind; for generations the Russian Church had
taught her members these doctrines, but at the same time it had
insisted that the new order could be realised only through the
willing obedience of men to God's rule, and as the result of their
moral regeneration.

The Communists radically rejected this side of the traditional
teaching, and at the same time promised to their followers quick
results and resounding victory. The weapons they advocated were
class struggle, severe party discipline, and the destruction of all
those opposed to their ardent faith. There were many in Russia
who could not accept this part of their doctrine, and the most
prominent among them were the Orthodox Christians.

There has been long and persistent misunderstanding in the
West as to the causes of the conflict between the Communist State
and the Russian Church. The lack of knowledge about the
character of Russian Christianity, the deep-rooted prejudice against
Eastern Orthodoxy, and skilfully conducted propaganda have all
contributed to the impression that the Christians in Russia suffered
at the hands of a revolutionary Government because of their
close association with the old Empire, and as the result of their
ignorance, superstitions and manifold corruptions. The true cause
of the struggle was quite different.

The majority of clergy and the bulk of the laity belonged to the
poorer classes in Russia before the Revolution. The privileged
and the well-to-do seldom showed any interest in Church life.
There was therefore no ground for Church opposition to the

economic and social reforms introduced by the Communists. The clash occurred on account of the radical difference between the Christian and the Marxian teaching on God and man.[1] The Communist assertion that there is no higher power than man led logically to the conclusion that the use of violence and compulsion is justified if its aim is the promotion of the common good. Moral laws are treated as entirely man-made and therefore they can be changed in accordance with the needs of the moment. This doctrine stands in irreconcilable opposition to Christian teaching that man's conduct is conditioned by Divine ordinance, and that its violation brings with it suffering and disruption. The whole outlook of the Russian people, shaped by the tradition of Eastern Orthodoxy, has always been antagonistic to acts of violence, and mistrustful of human effort unaided by Divine grace. There was, however, a section of Russian people ready to accept the tenets of Marxism, and to impose this theory upon the rest of the country. This was the minority of the Westernised Russians and the revolutionary representatives of the large Jewish population. Since the time of Peter the Great, the upper-class Russians had lost contact with the bulk of their people. Uprooted from their native soil, they looked upon Europe as the only source of truth and enlightenment. For them every new idea from the West was the last word in wisdom. This explains why the intellectuals of the country, where proletariat and capitalists in the Marxian sense of these words hardly existed at all, were the first to embrace wholeheartedly the Communist teaching that the industrial proletariat was the new Messiah, and that the blood of the capitalists alone could redeem the world from the sin of exploitation. European people, legally minded, property-conscious, and deeply affected by agnosticism, were afraid to risk their security and comfort. Sceptics and egoists do not make good revolutionaries; only those who are moved by faith can sacrifice what they possess for the sake of a better life for the next generation. The radicals among the Russians were not afraid to experiment, and their religious nature was stirred by the vision of a new earth purified from sin given to his followers by the founder of Communism. Neither were they disturbed by the price of great destruction, which, according to Karl Marx, mankind had to pay for entry into the realm of equality and freedom. The Russians were both attracted and repelled by European civilisation; they were fascinated by its

[1] The best study of the religious policy of the Communists in Russia is given in Professor N. Timasheff's book, *Religion in Soviet Russia*, London, 1943.

stability and self-confidence, and yet they despised it for its attachment to comfort and wealth. They, like Karl Marx, were outsiders whose roots belonged to another world, and they were prepared to blow up the whole imposing edifice in order to see how far the assertion made by Europeans that God was only the projection of their intellect, and that man could do what he liked, was really true.

The revolutionaries in Russia eagerly listened to the teaching that secularism was the final word in human progress, but in the depth of their hearts they were still doubtful. In order to verify this proposition, they decided to apply in practice the principles of atheism, and this was exactly what Western people, including the Socialists, were reluctant to do. Too many sentiments, fears and affections tied Western man to his cultural past. It would be distasteful to him to turn his cathedrals into museums, even though the majority had ceased to believe in God, to whose glory they were built. It would be unpleasant to stop speaking about progress and freedom, though these words had lost their original meaning. It would be painful to give up the hope of victory over selfishness and sin, though the very idea of sin was dismissed as old-fashioned, and any action which was not motivated by self-interest was ridiculed as sentimental and naïve. The European world needed radical reconstruction; its people had lived too long in a state of doubt and contradiction, and this had undermined their vitality and strength, but they could not break away from their old dreams, which many of them still hoped might yet come true. The Communists in Russia made this decisive step; they were not faint-hearted, they were ready to act according to the doctrine they professed. This gave the driving power to the movement, and enabled them to build up a new world.

The Communists in Russia did not believe in God, and therefore they were resolutely opposed to Christianity; they denied any future life, and they treated people accordingly; they refused to recognise any being higher than man, and therefore they ascribed to the collectivity, as represented by the leader of the party, absolute control over the individual. The Russian Revolution has a worldwide significance, but its message is primarily addressed to Western man, whose problems the Communists have tried so radically to solve. It marks the end of the long period of scepticism and religious confusion. It sets before mankind the inspiring task of establishing an integral social order, and it challenges all the conventions, customs and traditional beliefs on which the majority of European peoples had relied for two thousand years. There is no side of human life or activity which has not been tested or revised by the Communists. Politics, economics, science, education, family life, and the attitude to Nature, all underwent profound transformation; but behind all these changes the greatest and most formidable problem has been the question of the existence of God.

The Russian Revolution is man's greatest rebellion against the Creator. It is the final trial of man's ability and power to create here on earth, by his own efforts, the order which will satisfy all human needs and aspirations. The social experiment in Russia was made by those who had broken away irrevocably from every vestige of religion, and proclaimed that they were their own masters, responsible to no one for their conduct.

The daring social and economic reconstruction of the country, its amazing technical development, have been used by the Communists as a practical demonstration of the power possessed by godless men: a proof that Christ's teaching was a deception imposed upon the human race and that new and better social conditions could be achieved only by those who erased from their hearts and minds every trace of Christian tradition.

The Communists have shown that human beings can and should live in accordance with the doctrine they profess, and that an individual can find strength and satisfaction only in the service of a great and ennobling cause.

The Russians have also demonstrated that human endurance, readiness for self-sacrifice and the power of faith are far greater and far more dynamic than was admitted by de-Christianised and disillusioned modern man.

The Russian Revolution constitutes also an important step towards equality between Europe and Asia. It has awakened the Asiatic population of the U.S.S.R. and secured their full co-operation.

Dialectical materialism and political totalitarianism have been more generally accepted among the non-Christian people of the U.S.S.R. than among the Russians proper.[1] The rise in the cultural and economic standard has been particularly marked in the Asiatic districts. In these the emancipation of women from the restrictions imposed upon them by Mahometanism has been especially beneficial for society.

[1] U.S.S.R. is inhabited by more than a hundred different nationalities, who profess, besides Christianity, Judaism, Mahometanism, Buddhism, Shamanism and different pagan cults.

All these and many other achievements bear witness to the power given to collective man; they proclaim his mastery of natural forces, and his ability to direct them according to his will. But at the same time, the Communist experiment in Russia has disclosed the limitations of the godless man, and the most serious of these is his entire dependence on the use of mental and physical compulsion. Karl Marx preached the advent of equality and freedom to his followers. Lenin assured them that only by the determined use of every kind of violence, including terror, torture and lies, could men reach this promised land. With absolute faith in the words of their teachers, the Communists in Russia put these principles into practice. They were able by these means to industrialise the country, to build up a powerful modern army and to create hospitals, schools and research institutions. They spared neither material resources nor human life in carrying out these projects, but they are still far from the realm of happiness and freedom at which they originally aimed. Propaganda, prisons and concentration camps have eliminated much of the opposition, but they have not produced that regenerated man whose birth was prophesied by the founders of Communism.

For sceptics this is yet another proof that every hope of the radical improvement of human nature is only Utopianism. But for Christians it raises afresh the problem of how to establish a righteous life here on earth.

Communists and Christians have more in common than is òften realised. There is a greater gulf separating them from agnostics than that which parts them from each other; they both believe that mankind has its special task, and has the ability and power to fulfil it, but because they differ radically in their attitude to God, they use opposite weapons for the achievement of the ultimate goal. The Communist system bears the seal of its militant atheism and materialism in its ruthless treatment of individuals,[1] and subordination of all values to the economic interests of the collectivity.

It satisfies those who accept these tenets, but there is a large section of the Russian people who, after having experienced the godless rule, have reaffirmed their faith in the unique truth of

[1] Among many examples of ruthlessness, the law of April 7th, 1935, can be quoted. It was signed by Kalinin and Molotov, and authorised the Secret Police to condemn to death children who, having reached the age of twelve, commit crimes punishable by death in the case of adults. The Communists are keen to educate children, but if they do not fit into their system they are mercilessly destroyed.

Christ's teaching. The story of the struggle between them and the atheistic State awaits its full description. When all the facts are known, the Christian West will be amazed at the scope and the intensity of the contest. But those who conceive the defence of Christian truth along the lines of open resistance by a well-organised Church, under leaders defiant of State authorities, and boldly denouncing and condemning the ungodly, are bound to be disappointed at the conduct of the Christians in Russia. The Church there, weakened by two hundred years of bureaucratic control under the Empire of St. Petersburg, made at the beginning of the persecution some attempts at open resistance. These were ruthlessly crushed down, and never repeated. The external organisation of the Church collapsed almost at once. The bishops were arrested and scattered, the priests intimidated, the faithful systematically exiled and destroyed. Neither the clergy nor laity devised any plan of action; everybody was utterly bewildered and lost.

The Russian Revolution presents, therefore, the unique sight of a battle between the omnipotent State and a helpless Church. The attack of the State was directed by men of exceptional ability and strength of will, convinced of the truth of their doctrine, determined to destroy Christianity once and for all. They have used as their weapons the best organised police force in the world. They secured complete control of education, press and propaganda, and they were ready to apply every form of compulsion and intimidation against the believers. Their opponent was a paralysed Church, whose members were mainly people of little education and of low social standing. It is difficult to imagine two adversaries more unequal in power and status. Humanly speaking, the issue of the struggle was settled before the contest was even started. The doom of the Church was pronounced by many foreign observers, who declared that Christianity in Russia had not a single chance of survival.

But a strange thing has happened. The Communists, armed with all modern weapons, have launched one attack after another against their prostrate enemy, and yet, to their own amazement, they could not quench the life of this impotent body. The Church of Russia, without leaders, organisation or programme, has remained invincible and steadfast.[1] It was crushed down and yet

---

[1] These lines were written before the restoration of the Patriarchate in Moscow in September, 1943. This event serves as a further illustration of the vitality of Russian Christianity.

undestroyed; it was molested and tortured, but remains alive, and even retains an astonishing power of recuperation. Its members no longer attempt open resistance. The only thing they refuse to abandon is their faith in Christ, for they realise that without Him life has no purpose, and that no sacrifice really matters so long as one is in communion with Him.

This means that the daring predictions of the Russian prophets have been confirmed. The Russian Christians have acted as it was foretold they would act. They have demonstrated to the world that the strength of the Church lies, not in the ability of its leaders, not in their learning, not in organisation, but solely and uniquely in personal knowledge of Christ. For as long as Church members are in communion with Him, every one of them is a living example of Christ's victory over disunity, disease and death, and there is no power on earth or in heaven which can separate these human beings from the source of Divine life. The atheists in Russia have been defeated because they met a force which is stronger than man. All those things which are human in the life of the Church they destroyed at one stroke, but when they expected the Church to collapse as the result of their easy victory, their hopes were frustrated, for they were confronted no longer by men and man-built organisation, but by the Church of the Living God, reduced to its true function of uniting its members round the celebration of the Holy Eucharist, and of giving them there personal experience of Christ's life.[1] The Christians of Russia have been tested by one of the hardest of all trials, the sense of being abandoned and forgotten by all. Yet they were not fighting only their own battle, for the conflicts, doubts and contradictions of the whole history of the Church were brought to their climax in the tense struggle between them and the atheistic State.

In spite of divisions, the destiny of the Church is the same in all parts of the world, the success or failure of one of its sections means victory or defeat for the rest of the body. The Russian Christians, therefore, performed a service for all. They

[1] The anti-religious legislation of U.S.S.R. since 1929 has authorised only one activity for the believers, and this is worship. All educational, cultural and philanthropic work was forbidden. From the point of view of an atheist, worship of a non-existent god is the most useless of all human activities, and therefore it is tolerated by a godless State, but from a Christian point of view it is the most vital function of man, and, because the worship of the Russian Church is centred round the Eucharist, this divinely-appointed medicine for sin and corruption, its continuous performance has had far-reaching and beneficial consequences for Russian Christians.

revealed the Church's true source of power, they exposed the demonic character of secular Utopianism and at the same time they reaffirmed the importance of the social problem with which totalitarianism confronts the modern world. Man has a mission here on earth, but he can accomplish it only in co-operation with his Creator. Thus the Russian Church has fulfilled the role ascribed to it by the Russian thinkers; but there is another part of their prophecy still awaiting its confirmation. They were convinced that Christians would realise one day that they were called to transform the earth, under God's guidance, into His and man's perfect Kingdom.

Besides the road of death and resurrection, there is another and even more excellent way, the way of transfiguration. Christ revealed it before His Passion, when He appeared to His disciples in the company of Moses and Elijah, who according to the Biblical tradition, were both exempted by God from the trial of death.

The Russian Church, with its special love for the Feast of Transfiguration, has been more alive than others to the challenging message of this often misunderstood event of Christ's life. Its members, however, are unable to approach the task of transfiguring mankind and the rest of Nature in their present state of divisions, for only the reintegrated Church can be used by the Holy Spirit as a proper instrument for this purpose. The Russian prophets were acutely conscious of this, and hence their emphasis on unity, which left such a prominent mark on all their writings. They believed that inasmuch as the confusion as to the Church's true mission facilitated the growth of divisions among Christians, so the recovery of its right understanding will bring about the restoration of visible unity among them.

Their hope for reunion depended neither on doctrinal compromise nor on ecclesiastical reorganisation, but on the revival of trust in the Holy Spirit, who alone could heal the wounds inflicted upon the body of the Church by men haunted by fear of their own freedom and enslaved by their unbelief and pride. The œcumenical fellowship among Christians could never be based on any man-made pattern. It could only be inspired by the new life given to them through the Holy Eucharist.

Christians stand to-day at the cross-roads; the future of civilisation is dark and uncertain; its imposing edifice is threatened by the rising tide of secularism and militant atheism, and the number of those who are ready to defend it is small and inadequate for the task. Many experts have given their advice as to the best way of conducting the campaign, but none of their plans sounds convincing, and Christians remain paralysed by their rivalries and suspicions. At this moment of acute tension, the voice of three Russian writers resounds with authority and knowledge, for they were not, like many false prophets, unaware of the coming crisis. They had a clear grasp of its deep causes, and therefore they were able to give timely warning of its approach. They had no illusions about the degree of suffering and horror which it was bound to bring into the life of mankind, but they were not dismayed, for they were certain that a reunited Church could be properly armed for resistance to the iron rule of those who deny God and enslave man—the crown of His Creation.

The Russian writers addressed their message of Christian hope and freedom primarily to contemporary Churchmen in Russia, but their advice was dismissed as the words of eccentrics. Russia's fate in the twentieth century would have been very different if the rulers of the country had shown confidence in the prophetic voice of their great Christian thinkers. In our days the destiny of the whole Christian civilisation is at stake; its future will depend on its acceptance or rejection of the vision of the Church as seen by Khomiakov, Soloviev and Dostoevsky.

APPENDIX

BIBLIOGRAPHY

Chapter One. THE RUSSIAN BACKGROUND

The cultural background of Russia, and especially the influence of the Orthodox Church, were little studied before the Revolution. The predominant tendency among Westernised Russians was to treat their native culture as the remnant of a dead past, and the Church as the religion of an uneducated peasantry. The reaction from this point of view started only at the beginning of the twentieth century, but the process of rediscovery of Russia's cultural inheritance was interrupted by the Communist Revolution. The anti-religious policy pursued by the new Government made impossible the publication of any work appreciative of Russia's Christian tradition.

In the period 1918–39 the study of Russian religion could be carried on therefore only among the Russians in exile. Several important books were published in Russian in Berlin, and later in Paris by the Y.M.C.A. Press, but only few of them have yet appeared in any of the Western languages. The books on Russian culture and its Christian tradition available in English are the following:

ANON. *The Way of a Pilgrim.* Ed. French. London, 1941.
ARSENIEV, N. *Holy Moscow.* London, 1940.
BARING, M. *The Russian People.* London, 1914.
—— *The Mainsprings of Russia.* London, 1914.
BUXTON, D. *Russian Mediaeval Architecture.* Cambridge, 1934.
GORODETSKY, N. *The Humiliated Christ in Modern Russian Thought.* London, 1938.
GRAHAM, STEPHEN. *Undiscovered Russia.* London, 1912.
—— *With the Russian Pilgrims in Jerusalem.* London, 1913.
—— *The Way of Martha and the Way of Mary.* London, 1916
FRERE, W. *Some Links in the Chain of Russian Church History.* London, 1918.

JARINTZOV, N. *The Russians and their Language*. Oxford, 1916.
—— *Russia the Country of Extremes*. London, 1914.
LEROY-BEAULIEU, A. *L'Empire des Tzars et les Russes*. Paris, 1897-8.
　Available in English translation.
MASARYK, T. *The Spirit of Russia*. London, 1915.
MAYNARD, JOHN. *Russia in Flux*. London, 1941.
NEWMARCH, ROSA. *The Devout Russian*. London, 1918.
RILEY, A. (editor). *Birkbeck and the Russian Church*. London, 1917.
Russian Letters of Direction (Macarius of Optino, 1834–60). London,
　1944.
STEPHENS, W. (editor). *The Soul of Russia*. London, 1916.
WALLACE, D. MACKENZIE. *Russia*. London, 1912.
WILBOIS, J. *Russia and Reunion*. London, 1918.
WILLIAMS, W. *Russia of the Russians*. New York, 1914.
ZERNOV, N. *Moscow, the Third Rome*. London, 1942.
—— *St. Sergius: Builder of Russia*. London, 1939.
—— *The Russians and their Church*. London, 1944.

Chapter Two. KHOMIAKOV

Khomiakov's complete works were published in Russian in 1900 in eight volumes.
His theological articles are available in French.

KHOMIAKOV. *L'Eglise Latine et le Protestantisme*. Lausanne, 1872.
　The best study of his life and thought is also in French.
GRATIEUX, A. *A. S. Khomiakov*. Vols. I and II. Paris, 1939.
　Very little of his work has been translated into English.
KHOMIAKOV. *The Orthodox Doctrine on the Church*. Brussels, 1864.
BIRKBECK, W. J. *Russia and the English Church during the Last Fifty
　Years*. Vol. I. London, 1895. Contains Khomiakov's correspon-
　dence with W. Palmer.

Chapter Three. DOSTOEVSKY

Dostoevsky's works, with the exception of most of *The Journal of an Author*, are available in English. Selections from the *Journal* have been edited by Middleton Murry. The best studies of Dostoevsky in English are:

BERDYAEV, N. *Dostoevsky*. London, 1934.
CARR, E. *Dostoevsky*. London, 1931.
LAVRIN, J. *Dostoevsky*. London, 1943.
LLOYD, J. A. T. *A Great Russian Realist*. London, 1912.
MAURINA, Z. *A Prophet of the Soul*. —, 1940.

MURRY, J. MIDDLETON. *Fyodor Dostoevsky*. London, 1923.
SIMMONS, E. J. *Dostoevsky*. New York, 1940.

Chapter Four. SOLOVIEV

Soloviev's complete works were published in Moscow in 1911 in ten volumes.
Only a few of them have been translated into English:

War and Christianity. London, 1915.
War, Progress and the End of History. London, 1915.
The Justification of the Good. Tr. Duddington. London, 1918.
God, Man and the Church. Tr. Attwater. London, 1935.
Plato. Tr. Lavrin. London, 1935.

Among the few books on Soloviev the following can be mentioned:

D'HERBIGNY, M. *Vladimir Soloviev, a Russian Newman*. London, 1918.
PFLEGER. *Wrestlers with Christ*. London, 1937.
STREMOUKHOFF. *Vladimir Soloviev et son Œuvre Messianique*. Paris, 1935.

Chapter Five. THE FUTURE OF CHRISTIAN CIVILISATION

For further study of the problem raised in this chapter, the following books can be recommended:

ANDERSON P. *People, Church and State in Modern Russia*. London, 1944.
BERDYAEV, N. *The Russian Revolution*. London, 1931.
—— *Christianity and the Class War*. London, 1933.
—— *The End of Our Time*. London, 1933.
—— *The Fate of Man in the Modern World*. London, 1935.
—— *The Meaning of History*. London, 1936.
—— *The Destiny of Man*. London, 1937.
—— *The Origin of Russian Communism*. London, 1937.
DAWSON, C. *The Judgment of the Nations*. London, 1943.
DAVIES, D. R. *On to Orthodoxy*. London, 1939.
—— *The Two Humanities*. London, 1940.
MANNHEIM, K. *Diagnosis of Our Time*. London, 1943.
MURRY, J. MIDDLETON. *The Necessity of Communism*. London, 1939.
NERSOYAN, T. *A Christian Approach to Communism*. London, 1942.
TIMASHEFF, N. S. *Religion in Soviet Russia*. London, 1943.
VIDLER, A. *God's Judgment on Europe*. London, 1940.
VOIGT, F. A. *Unto Cæsar*. London, 1938.